# VIEW

*Cover designs by* Grange Hill *fans*

## I'M BROKE

In the last annual, you asked if we readers think that the magazines and novels are a fair reflection of the television series, and whether they are good value for money.

Well, I do think they are like the show, but they should have more pictures in COLOUR! Also, I don't think the magazines and annuals are good value for money. Over £2.00 for an annual is too much—I can only afford to pay about £1.50.

***Tracey Lemon, Chesham.***

*Point taken, Tracey, but I'm afraid that I cannot make the annuals any cheaper. Photographs, illustrations, production costs, paper and printing all cost an awful lot of money. Even when an annual is printed, it still has to be distributed around the country to newsagents and retail shops, which means more money to pay out.*

*Would readers prefer an annual with less pages and not so much ... a cheaper price?—Phil.*

## WE'RE CONFUSED

My younger sister and I are very confused. In the first series of **Grange Hill,** Tucker and Trisha were meant to be in the first year. I was in the first year too, but when they reached the fifth year, I'd only got to the fourth. Can you explain?

***Tracy Wright, Nottingham.***

*Although life in the series is similar to real-life, it is not real-life. I write about the first, third and fifth years only—which means that sometimes characters move up to a new year rather more quickly than would really happen—Phil.*

## SO HAPPY

My name is Bernadette Deevoy and I am writing to thank you for the strength and courage you gave me through your wonderful series **Grange Hill.**

When I started in the first year of my secondary school, I found it very strange. Unable to fit in, I became very unhappy—until I started watching **Grange Hill.** It reminded me of my own problems and helped me to solve them. I started taking part in school activities and attending music and drama lessons where I met lots of nice people. My ambition now is to act in **Grange Hill** because the show inspired me so much.

Love and best wishes!

***Bernie, N. Ireland.***

## HALF A SHOW

Last Christmas I was very upset. The special Christmas edition of **Grange Hill** was being shown and I'd really been looking forward to it. Halfway through though, the picture on my television went off and it didn't come back on again. Some transmitter had broken down or something. Can you possibly show it again?

***Linda Reid, Bolton.***

*The BBC already have, Linda. I hope you weren't unlucky enough to miss it twice—Phil.*

## PLEASE REPEAT!

I've just thought of a great idea! Lots of kids I know were too young to really understand **Grange Hill** when it was first shown as they were only about five. Now they're really interested however, and would love to see the series right from the beginning. Couldn't you start the show from the very first part during the summer? Come on, how about it?

***Janice Peters, London.***

## WELL DONE!

The **Grange Hill Annual 1982** was well worth £2.50 because it was superb in every way. I enjoyed the quizzes and stories very much and thought the pin-ups were good. Thank you for putting so much useful information inside!

***Samantha Westley, Kent.***

## GREAT COLLECTION

I'm a mad **Grange Hill** collector! I've got the magazines, annuals, novels, diaries, exercise books and lots of other bits and pieces. All my mates are madly jealous. (Shame!)

Are you bringing out anything else with **Grange Hill?** Please let me know!

***Cathy Jones, Bristol.***

*Actually, I am working on many other ideas for **Grange Hill** products. There's a bike, rubbers, pencils, a lunch-box, sweets, a watch . . . the list is quite long.*

*If you have any suggestions for other things that could be given the **Grange Hill** stamp, describe them in a letter. I'll be very interested—Phil.*

A Grange Hill Story
THE CHiPS ARE DOWN
Heley
GREENGROCERY SPECIALS
FOOD PRICES
BLIMEY, IT'S MURDER IN THERE! LAST TIME I DO MUM'S SHOPPING!
FIRST TIME AND ALL, ISN'T IT? WHAT'VE YOU GOT TO MOAN ABOUT?
It was Saturday morning . . . and two *Grange Hill* inmates had been lumbered!
FANCY SOME GRUB? I'M STARVING!
HAVEN'T ANY MONEY!
WHAT DO YOU CALL THIS, THEN?
IT'S MY MUM'S CHANGE! CAN'T SPEND THAT!
NO NEED TO SPEND ALL OF IT, IS THERE? MAKE OUT YOU LOST SOME!
NO WAY! I COULDN'T, ANNETTE!
WHAT'S THE MATTER . . . SCARED OF YOUR MUM OR SOMETHING?
WELL, SHE'S NOT AS SOFT AS YOUR MUM! I DON'T GET AWAY WITH THE THINGS YOU DO!

TELL YOU WHAT, SINCE YOU'RE SO SCARED, I'LL PAY!
OH, I WASN'T ASKING YOU TO DO THAT!
WELL, I'M NOT EATING ON MY OWN! COME ON!
So . . .
DUNNO ABOUT YOU, BUT I'M HAVING COD AND CHIPS AND A COKE!
BLIMEY! I'M NOT HAVING ALL THAT!
But . . .
TWO COD AND CHIPS . . . AND TWO COKES!
GO ON! YOU'LL MANAGE IT, WON'T YOU?
ANYTHING YOU DON'T WANT, CHUCK IT OVER HERE!
RECKON I'LL COPE!
THIS IS GREAT . . . HEY, WHAT'S WRONG?
BLIMEY! DIDN'T EXPECT IT TO COME TO SO MUCH!

TWO POUND THIRTY! I HAVEN'T GOT ENOUGH CASH LEFT!
WHAT ARE WE GOING TO DO?
ONLY ONE THING WE CAN DO . . . WE'LL HAVE TO DIP INTO YOUR CHANGE!
OH, NO. . .
Fay didn't have any choice . . .
QUALITY
YOU KNEW YOU HADN'T ENOUGH MONEY WHEN WE WENT IN THERE!
'COURSE I DIDN'T!
ANYWAY, YOU WERE HAPPY ENOUGH SPENDING MY MUM'S MONEY, WEREN'T YOU!
FORTY PENCE SHORT! MUM'LL GO MAD!
FORGET IT! SHE WON'T EVEN NOTICE!
YOU DON'T KNOW MY MUM! SHE CHECKS EVERY PENNY!
SOMEHOW, I'VE GOT TO GET THAT MONEY BACK BEFORE I GET HOME!
WHAT YA GONNA DO . . . BEG FOR IT?
HEY, WHERE ARE YOU GOING?
I'M GOING TO EARN IT, SAME WAY OTHER KIDS DO!

CLEAN YOUR CAR FOR YOU, MISTER?
NO THANKS! I CLEAN IT MYSELF!
DON'T DO A VERY GOOD JOB OF IT, DO YA!
WHAT?
CLEAR OFF, YOU TWO. GO ON — HOPPIT!
THANKS FOR NOTHING!
YOU CAN GO HOME, IF YOU LIKE! I'LL MANAGE BETTER ON MY OWN!
AW, COME ON, FAY! FORGET IT!
But this time . . .
FORTY PENCE FOR A WASH AND SHINE!
TWENTY! TAKE IT OR LEAVE IT!
JUST STAND THERE LOOKING STUPID, WHY DON'T YOU?
TWENTY PENCE? YOU MUST BE SOFT!
NO NEED TO BE TOO FUSSY, IS THERE!
LOOK, SHOVE OFF! DON'T WORRY ABOUT ME!

OH . . . GIMME A CLOTH! OR WE'LL BE HERE ALL DAY!
HUH!
Soon . . .
THERE! NOT BAD, EH?
RIGHT, LET'S GO AND GET YOUR MONEY!
YOU'VE DONE A GOOD JOB, GIRLS!
WORTH MORE THAN 20p!
ANNETTE!
OKAY, I'LL MAKE IT TWENTY-FIVE.
THANKS A LOT!
*HOW GENEROUS CAN YOU GET?*
I'M ONLY 15p SHORT NOW!
WHAT'S 15p? YOU'RE NOT GOING TO LET THAT WORRY YOU?
ANOTHER CAR'LL DO IT! WON'T TAKE LONG!
BLIMEY! YOU **ARE** A NUTJOB!

I'VE HAD ENOUGH, I'M GOING!
FINE! SEE YOU LATER!
An hour went by . . .
BACK TO SQUARE ONE! NOTHING TO FEEL GUILTY ABOUT NOW!
BLIMEY! HAVEN'T YOU GONE HOME YET?
NOPE, BUT I'VE GOT ALL THE MONEY!
WHAT DID YOUR MUM SAY ABOUT NOT GETTING HER CHANGE?
HALF-BELIEVED I'D DROPPED IT OUT OF MY POCKET! STILL GOT A TELLING OFF, THOUGH — NOTHING SERIOUS!
I'LL POP ROUND LATER!
TALK ABOUT HAVING POTS OF JAM!!
Back home . . .
THAT YOU BACK? WHERE HAVE YOU BEEN ALL THIS TIME?
SHOP WAS PACKED! HAD TO QUEUE!

DON'T GIVE ME THOSE LIES! I KNOW WHERE YOU'VE BEEN . . .
EH?
. . . STUFFING YOUR FACE IN SOME CAFE WITH THAT ANNNETTE FIRMAN! YOUR BROTHER SAW YOU!
WHAT I WANT TO KNOW IS . . . WHERE DID THE MONEY COME FROM?
ANNETTE PAID FOR IT ALL!
CAME OUT OF MY CHANGE, MORE LIKE!
AREN'T YOU EVEN GOING TO CHECK IT?
WHAT'S THE POINT? GO TO YOUR ROOM . . .
BUT, OH . . . NEVER MIND.
WHAT'S THE USE TRYING TO EXPLAIN? IF I'D SAID ANY MORE, I'D ONLY HAVE LANDED MYSELF DEEPER IN IT!
THE END

# GET TO GRIPS WITH GRAPHOLOGY!

THIS IS VERY HANDY!

LEARN SOMETHING NEW!

**Next time that dog-eared exercise book of yours comes back, with "Good try" or "Careless work!" scrawled on it by your teacher, don't just sling it back into your desk! Handwriting can tell you a lot about people! Every detail—the spacing and slope of the words, the size and slant of the writing, can mean something. So suss out your teachers this way!**

A If you can't find Miss (A), try the broom cupboard or book store-room! Those large, regular spaces between her words show she prefers to be alone! A writer who leaves no spaces between words likes to be in a group. And what about irregular, varying spaces? They indicate someone vague and excitable, who can't control their feelings! So don't be surprised if a teacher with such writing forgets to set homework, then weeps inconsolably because no one did any!

*See me later*

B Oh-oh! Even if Mr. (B) starts by promising you no homework, he may dole out a double helping at the end of the lesson! That wavering line shows he's an excitable, unreliable type, subject to sudden mood changes!

*your spelling is hopeless*

C Don't bother trying to tell Mrs. (C) the dog chewed up your homework! She's not quite the pushover you may think! Small writing like hers shows someone shy and modest—but also shrewd and perceptive!

*very nice neat writing indeed...*

D Mr. (D) is Superman—large writing, if even and well-controlled, shows an outgoing, enterprising person with natural superiority and great willpower. But beware if large writing is wild and careless—it reveals a show-off!

*improve yourself*

E Miss (E) is the athletic, outdoor type! The long lower loops of her writing show a person interested in the physical things of life!

*you played great*

F Mr. (F) is the one who always comes to the school fancy dress do as Napoleon, and dances a Highland Fling—during the waltz! His extremely right-slanting writing reflects delusions of grandeur and unrestrained behaviour!

*A superb effort!!*

G Not the best bet for a special favour or request! Mr. (G)'s left-slanting writing indicates someone who always opposes everything. The writer is withdrawn, unadaptable and detached!

*ridiculous opinions*

H There's nothing Mrs. (H) likes better than giving orders and laying down the law—you can tell by the heaviness of those final downstrokes of her words! But if *all* downstrokes are heavy, the writer is self-centred and over-ambitious! Light pressure says someone is quiet and modest but alert and active!

*See me now*

I Woe betide you if Mr. (I) takes one of his instinctive dislikes to *you!* Those constantly separated letters of his are the sign of an imaginative, creative and unsociable person who tends to jump to conclusions and make hasty decisions based on instinct and intuition. Someone who links *all* his letters is a careful, practical type.

*I feel you did not try at all*

J Mr. (J) just loves to please, and tries to curry favour and make himself popular! Those downward-curving curly stokes at the start of each of his words show a crawling quality. An upcurling initial stroke (first letters of words) show he resents interference! Final letters are also revealing. A well-proportioned one shows the writer to be trustworthy, practical and not easily deceived!

*Brilliant Work*

**★ Of course, we haven't turned you into a handwriting expert! We've simply explained most of the basic points to note—size of writing, width, slope, slant, pressure, spacing etc. If you're seriously interested in graphology, there are some good and inexpensive paperbacks available on the subject. You're not? Never mind, just grab an exercise book—or copy an example of your teacher's writing from the board—and use the tips we've given you to have some very revealing fun!**

A Grange Hill Story

# A Right Spectacle!

**Tucker in glasses? It had to be a joke! Perhaps he was taking the rise out of some teacher. That must be it!**

"Peter! Glasses!"

**The words grated on Tucker Jenkins' eardrums for the hundredth time that week. His mum never tired of saying them. Whenever she saw him within reading distance of a magazine or viewing distance of a television screen, they sprang to her lips.**

It was no use ignoring her. She'd switch the telly off or grab his magazine until he'd obeyed. And if that didn't work, she'd repeat her catchphrase like a scratched record until his dad was driven to lend his support.

"You heard your mother," he'd end up snarling. "Or do you need a hearing aid as well?"

Flaming specs, Tucker muttered, plodding to his room to fetch them. I don't even need them. There's nothing wrong with my eyesight. It's the last time I'll ever go to a doctor about a headache.

It was his mum that had made him go. He'd had a succession of real skull-splitters and aspirins didn't seem to be doing the trick. He put it down to too many late nights in front of the box. Then his mum stepped in and made an appointment with the doctor.

Next thing he knew, he'd been bundled off to have his eyes tested by some dumpy little gnome with double-glazed goggles in St. Mary's Lane. How he ever became an optician, Tucker would never know. He even tripped over Mum's handbag on the way to the wall chart.

Anyway, that didn't stop him deciding that Tucker's eyes were less than perfect. The choice of frames was awful, so Tucker chose one of the cheapest designs and resolved never to wear them. Two weeks later, the silver-rimmed eyesores were ready for collection. Knowing that Tucker would delay picking them up, Mrs. Jenkins called round for them.

"They suit you!" she'd beamed after making him try them on for the twentieth time. "Make you look quite intelligent!" This worried Tucker.

"Know who you remind me of . .?" was his dad's initial reaction. He grinned as he peeped from behind his paper. ". . . the Two Ronnies!"

"What, *both of 'em?*" Tucker scowled. He might have known there'd be some stupid remarks!

What really hurt was the fact that

***The steam on Tucker's lenses shrouded the world in mist whenever he leant down and sipped his coffee!***

his headaches had vanished the day after he saw the doc. A week before he went to see the optician. But by then it was too late. The wheels were in motion.

This particular evening, he'd gone and put the things on for the sake of peace and quiet while he watched Steve McQueen performing motorbike heroics for the millionth time in *The Great Escape*. The film didn't look any different when viewed through glass, except that steam on the lenses shrouded the whole thing in mist whenever he sipped his coffee.

So caught up was he in the action that he didn't even hear the doorbell ring. The first he knew of it was when his mum ushered Alan Humphries into the room.

"Blimey!" Alan exploded as Tucker turned in alarm, as if he'd been caught shoplifting. "I didn't know it was fancy dress night!"

Tucker's mum caught the gist of things right away.

"Surely you've seen his spectacles before now," she queried, her suspicions roused. "He's been wearing them at school, hasn't he?" She wheeled to face a worried Tucker. "Haven't you?"

"Well . . . yeah! 'Course he has. I was only joking," Alan burbled, trying to get Tucker out of a fix.

***"I don't have to go round shouting about it," Alan said. "Everyone will see your goggles for themselves soon enough!"***

But Tucker's expression had given the game away.

"Trust you to turn up like that," he nagged Alan later on, as he saw him to the door. "Couldn't the stupid homework have waited?"

Alan grinned and dug him in the ribs. "You're only narked 'cos I found out! See ya, four eyes!" And he strolled off, turning to make binoculars with his hands.

Tucker slammed the door and cursed his luck.

Next morning, he felt like bunking off school, but he knew it was pointless. He had to go in sometime and face the music. And his mum had blown her top already about him not wearing his specs in class, so he didn't want to make things worse.

Surprisingly, on the bus trip to *Grange Hill*, Alan made it clear he wasn't going to spread the news. He made plenty of jokes about it just to watch Tucker squirm, but he was quite offended when Tucker accused him of having a big mouth.

"I don't have to go round shouting about it," he pointed out. "Everyone will see your goggles for themselves when you put them on."

Tucker soon put him in the picture. Although his mum had made sure that he'd taken his specs with him, he still had no intention of wearing them. He was sure he could count on Al's support if she asked him about them again, couldn't he? She wasn't likely to see anyone else to interrogate.

All this intrigue worried Tucker more than he cared to admit. He liked

***All eyes were on him. His world crashed around his ears for a few seconds before he recovered himself.***

life to be nice and simple. Since he'd got his specs, it had become too complicated for comfort. He had to be constantly on his guard against most people finding out that he did wear specs and against his mum finding out that he didn't.

What's more, he didn't feel as confident as he used to. Before, he felt pretty secure at *Grange Hill*. No-one could really get at him. But now that had changed. He felt vulnerable and it wasn't a nice feeling.

That first morning after Alan found out, Tucker noticed something else.

It hit him when he and Alan strolled into the playground to join Tommy Watson who was taking the mickey out of Stammers Chalmers,

the only kid who could turn a few words into a life sentence.

"Aw, leave him alone," Tucker mumbled. He didn't care about Chalmers. He was a creep, regardless of his impediment, but Tucker could see himself getting a bad time once it was known that he wore specs.

Tommy stuttered to a halt and gave Alan a strange look. "What's up with him?" he asked, indicating Tucker who was sloping off. Alan just shrugged and said nothing. Specs seemed to be changing Tucker's attitudes even when he wasn't wearing them.

After registration, the class rose to go to their first lesson. Suddenly Mr. Sutcliffe remembered something.

"Oh . . . Peter," he said to Tucker. "Don't forget to wear your specs!" He smiled and wagged a finger.

In a flash, all eyes were on Tucker. His world crashed around his ears for a few seconds before he recovered himself.

Nipping smartly from the room with leering faces hurling questions at him, he fobbed them off.

"Look, it's Sooty's idea of a joke, I'm telling ya," he snapped, wondering how Sutcliffe had found out. Alan? Naw, surely not. His mum?

All was revealed in the next lesson. As soon as the work had been handed out, Miss Peterson approached Tucker's desk.

"I believe you're meant to wear spectacles, Peter," she said crisply.

Colour rushed to Tucker's cheeks. Blimey, they all knew!

"Don't look so puzzled," she went on. "Your mother telephoned the school this morning. She can read you like a book."

Astonished smiles spread across the room. Trisha Yates and Cathy Hargreaves started to giggle. Tucker turned on them all.

"Shurrup, Pongo!"

"That will do, Peter. Now . . . spectacles!"

Miss Peterson stood waiting as he fumbled in his case.

"Sorry, Miss . . . must've left 'em at home," he pleaded, all innocence.

***The next few days were torture. Doyle, Trisha Yates, Cathy Hargreaves. . .they all had it in for him.***

"Not according to your mother," she replied, opening his case and pointing inside. "Surely, your eyesight isn't that bad!"

Howls of laughter filled the air, followed by a roar as Tucker blushingly produced the specs and put them on. He kept his head as low as possible over his desk so no-one could get a good look. Miss Peterson had never seen him look so studious.

"There's no need to get all steamed up about it," Alan told Tucker after he had endured a whole lesson of constant leg-pulling. "I thought you could take a joke!"

"Who says I can't?" Tucker growled, looking forward to sticking one on Mike Doyle, his chief tormentor. "Anyway, it's easy for you to laugh! You don't have to wear 'em!"

"Aw, poor likkle Tucker!" Alan cooed. "Feeling ever so sorry for himself, is he?"

"Oh, get stuffed!"

Tucker stormed off to the next lesson on his own.

The next few days were just as bad. Each lesson was torture. Doyle, Trisha Yates, Cathy Hargreaves . . . they all had it in for him. Boys, Tucker could deal with, but girls were another matter. He could hardly give them a knuckle sandwich.

At home, his parents noted his moodiness and father coaxed the truth out of him as they watched a late night film. His mother had gone to bed, so Tucker felt free to slate his specs and those who had lumbered him with them.

"The specs aren't the problem," his dad said, quite bluntly. "It's you."

Tucker thought about that for a few days and decided his dad was wrong. The specs were the problem, but he'd have to learn to live with them somehow. Just how came to him in a moment of inspiration. He dreamed up a great bluff . . .

Trisha Yates and Cathy Har-

***It was the first victory for Tucker's X-ray specs. By the end of the week, they were a privilege to wear.***

greaves were sniggering away at the back of the class again.

"Thinks he's Elvis Costello," was all Tucker heard.

He turned and leered at them. A long, ogling, penetrating stare through his hated silver specs.

"Gerroff, Jenkins. What're you staring at?" said Trisha, shifting uncomfortably on her chair.

Tucker removed his specs and handed them to Alan.

"Take a look," he grinned. "You can see right through that material!"

By now, others had joined in the game and the two girls buttoned their blazers.

It was the first victory for Tucker's X-ray specs. By the end of the week, they were celebrities in their own right. Wearing them was a privilege that few shared. Almost overnight, Tucker had become quite clearly attached to them.

Then his headaches suddenly reappeared. They were so bad, he reluctantly agreed to stay in bed.

"Anything new you've been eating?" enquired the doctor when he made his call.

"Not that I can think of," Tucker replied, lying propped up on pillows. What had all this got to do with his headaches? He hadn't been poisoned, had he?

"I'll have the results by the end of the week," he heard the doctor tell his mother as he left.

Tucker settled back to make the most of the situation and enjoy a week at home. He'd the colour television in his room, plenty of fruit and things to drink, comics galore and unlimited sympathy. Best of all, he hadn't had a headache for two days, though he wasn't going to tell anyone. Might as well have a week off school if he could get away with it.

"Is there anything else I can get you?" his mum asked before popping out to the shops.

"I suppose I could go a bar of chocolate," he ventured. "There's money in my trouser pocket."

"No, no. I'll stand you it," she said as she went out. Tucker smiled. He knew she would.

It was Friday when the doctor came back to see him—and not a moment too soon, Tucker groaned. Whatever it was that brought these headaches on, it had returned with a vengeance. His head throbbed like a drum.

"Good news," smiled the doctor. "I think we've solved the puzzle. What do you think we found?"

Tucker just wished he'd get on with it. He didn't feel up to playing guessing games.

"Dairy products! You've developed an allergy to them."

***He'd the colour television in his room, plenty of fruit, drinks, comics and unlimited sympathy!***

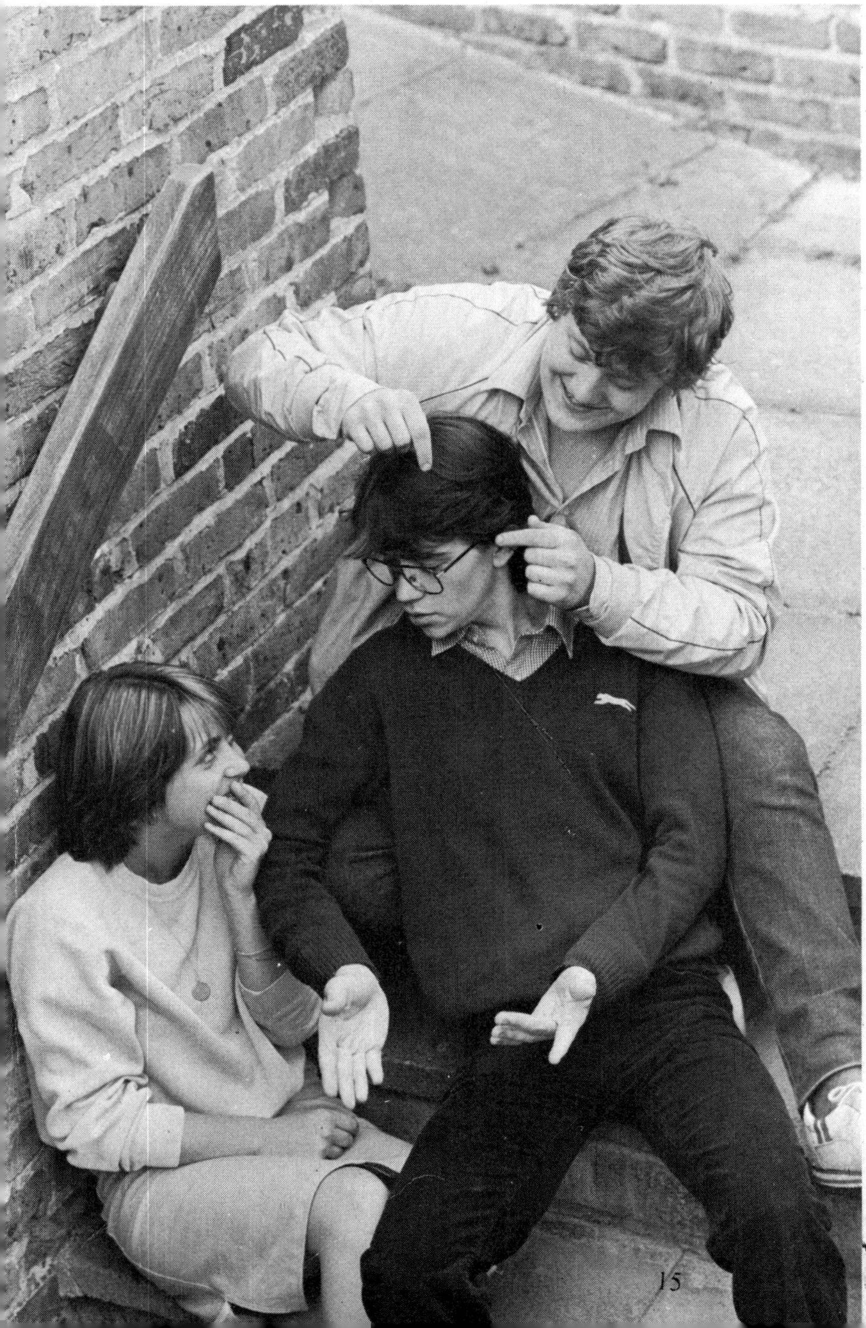

Tucker gaped at him. It took a while to sink in.

"You mean, I didn't need specs after all?"

"Well, I couldn't say that. But it's unlikely that eyestrain caused your headaches. This allergy is much more likely to have brought them on."

Oh, great! Tucker groaned. All that aggro. . .for nothing. And now this. . .dairy products. What would they be? Milk, cheese . . ?

"You won't be needing this, my lad," the doctor scolded, lifting something from the bedside table.

Tucker gasped. It was the extra chocolate bar his mum had bought him. What was wrong with it?

"Chocolate is out from now on, I'm afraid! Milk content, you see."

He handed the bar to Mrs. Jenkins who looked sympathetically at the figure on the bed. Poor Peter had had a hard time of it lately.

Tucker heard the front door close as his mother saw the doctor out. His headache hadn't got any better, and he'd been looking forward to that chocolate. His favourite treat—banned! They'd really think that was a laugh at *Grange Hill*. . .

**THE END**

STOP! LOOK! LISTEN!

## *How to tell when you've pushed your teacher too far!*

# ENUFF IS ENUFF!

**Push a teacher over the top and you're in trouble! So take a crash course right away in spotting the signs that spell DANGER!**

### *Things that push 'em over the top!*

A rule that applies to one teacher won't necessarily apply to another. Some will stretch like elastic, others lose their tempers and snap as easily as a stick of rock. Miss Jones might let you hum and whistle all through biology, whereas Mr. Smith goes crazy if you so much as cough during French.

Here are a few things that are guaranteed to annoy, niggle, irritate, anger, infuriate and even madden average teachers. (You'll probably be able to add to the list yourself . . .)

* Spelling enough as enuff!
* Talking when their back is turned.
* Talking when their back *isn't* turned.
* Holding your own lesson on what you did over the weekend while they're trying to tell you what Wellington did at Waterloo.
* Sniggering when they stutter.
* Saying, 'Hello, Dearie' when they walk in.
* Putting a whoopee cushion on their chair.
* Laughing out loud as they sit on it.
* Passing messages on paper aeroplanes.
* Always coming in late.
* Cheering when the bell goes at the end of the lesson.
* Flicking rubber bands across the room.
* Using the five minutes before the start of a lesson to do a life-like drawing of your teacher on the blackboard—big nose and all.
* Acting the mad professor in the lab and inventing a new type of stink bomb. Then letting it off.
* Not doing your homework.
* Knowing the answers to all their questions. (This often seems to annoy teachers more than anything—they think you must be cheating somehow!)

### *You know you've pushed a teacher much too far when. . .*

* They go down on their knees and beg you to change schools.
* Their neck turns bright red, steam comes out of the ears and their eyes bulge (even more than usual!)
* They have to rush out of the classroom and take a dive in the swimming pool to cool off.
* She/he sees you coming along the corridor—and faints/collapses.
* They buy you a Christmas present. A gag!
* Teach loses his/her voice from constantly shouting at you.
* They snap a ruler in half trying to restrain themselves from hitting you with it.
* You find a wax effigy of yourself on your desk, with pins stuck in it.
* The games teacher suggests they use you as the ball.
* Your classmates sitting near you start wearing crash helmets and goggles to protect them from stray pieces of flying chalk.
* You get threatened with detention—for the rest of your life!
* They have to get a new set of false teeth. All that gnashing has worn down the old ones.
* You come back after the summer holidays to find the school's closed down!
* You're asked to run an errand at the beginning of each lesson, and told 'not to hurry back'.
* He/she doesn't turn up for registration one morning and you hear they've had a nervous breakdown.

### *How to defuse an exploding teacher*

It might come as a surprise to learn this, but teachers are human too. If you think of them as enemies, imprisoning you all day and torturing you by making you listen to hours of boring facts and figures, imagine things from their point of view. For example, how would you like to be in charge of a group of thirty or forty pupils just like yourself?

Of course, a teacher gets paid for doing what he or she does, and you don't. But just the same, there's no point in deliberately being nasty to them for making you suffer. You don't have to go to the opposite extreme and start up a Society for the Prevention of Cruelty to Teachers—just learn their limits.

Little things please little minds and one intelligent question asked during a lesson will probably endear you to some teachers for life.

It doesn't involve being a creep or a pet pupil, and it can have the effect of getting them off the boring subject they're currently mumbling on about.

Teachers are also very suspicious by nature. If you like sitting at the back of the class, they're bound to suspect you of getting as far away from them as possible so you can chat through their lesson in peace.

Practise looking interested in front of a mirror. Screw up your eyes like you're concentrating, smile a bit as if you're enjoying yourself. Once you've perfected the technique, you can sit there through a lesson and the teacher will think you're all ears and attention, when in reality you're daydreaming, miles away.

It's easy to annoy teachers. It's also pretty easy *not* to. So why not stop getting up their noses and give you and them a break?!

**SAMUEL ZAMMO McGUIRE**
**(Lee MacDonald)**

BIRTHDAY: 21st June, 1968 STAR SIGN: Cancer
FAVOURITE FOOD: Fish and chips HOBBIES: Disco roller skating and reading good books
PETS: Five goldfish called Starsky and Hutch and Charlie's Angels BROTHERS: 1 younger, Dan SISTERS: None
OTHER APPEARANCES: In the film, *Memoirs of a Survivor, Noah's Castle* (Southern) and the series, *Squad* (Thames)

# THE FRENCH

*Alan was afraid that Susi's new friend would come between them. If Pierre was good-looking and full of French charm, he'd be a real threat. Little did he know there was absolutely nothing at all to worry about . . .*

**"A frog, coming to stay with you?"**

**The short question summed up Alan's attitude to Susi's news. She'd tried to pick the best moment to tell him, and he'd taken it as well as she'd expected. That is, badly. But he did have to be told.**

**"Don't blame me," she frowned. "It wasn't my idea. My mum arranged it. Thought it'd do my French some good."**

*The whole business made Alan more and more angry . . .*

"Well . . . the best of luck and all that," he shrugged. "S'pose that means you'll be busy most of the holidays."

"I'll have to look after him. Can't leave him on his own, can I?" She scraped her heels against the wall she was sitting on. "Maybe we can *both* show him around!" she said, hopefully, trying to smooth things out between them.

"Oh, yeah . . . great. There'll be you and him jabbering away in French and me stuck between you, like a flaming gooseberry!"

"Rubbish! Anyway, he's coming here to improve his English, so he'll be speaking that all the time, I expect."

"How's that gonna improve your French, then?"

"It won't until the summer. That's when I go over there to stay at his place. That's why they call it an exchange trip, see?"

## A Grange Hill Story

Alan didn't see. The whole business made him more and more angry. First, he wasn't going to see his girlfriend for the coming holiday, or most of it. Then he'd be stuck at home during the summer while she'd be getting chatted up by a walking language lab.

"Anyway," Susi snapped, fed up with his moodiness, "what's it to you? Not jealous, are you?"

"No chance," he sneered, rather too convincingly. "You can do what you blinkin' like for all I care!"

"Oh, very generous, I must say! Considering it's my life you're talking about. You don't own me, you know!" She could have bitten her tongue off the moment she said it.

"Get stuffed!" Alan said and walked off.

"And don't bother to call round!" she yelled after him, inflicting more pain on herself.

# CONNECTION

Tucker and Tommy were dead pleased when they heard about the row.

"Come to your senses at last, me old son," was Tucker's view of it. "You're better off without that stupid cow!"

It was the wrong thing to say. In a flash, Alan had him by the lapels.

"Watch it! That's my girlfriend you're talking about!" he snarled, his face red and twisted.

"Okay, okay! Blimey!" Tucker couldn't understand it. One minute he was against her, the next . . .

"When's Sacha Distel arriving then?" Tommy asked, trying to cool things down a bit.

"Sacha Distel?" Tucker laughed. "Showing your age a bit, aren't ya?" He turned to Alan who was slouching along, hands in pockets. "Expect he'll be arriving at Victoria, eh?" Alan didn't answer . . .

* * * * *

*It amused him to see how childish Pierre was—he still wanted to play dopey games!*

Ten days later, Susi and her mum were standing on the platform waiting for the boat train. They could see it approaching in slow motion. Susi eyed the open corridor windows as they edged past. Heads stuck out of them—passengers were preparing to throw themselves off at the first opportunity. She wondered which one was him?

She wasn't really looking forward to his arrival. She didn't like having acquaintanceships thrust upon her. She looked at her mother, eagerly scanning the carriages. Mrs. MacMahon was looking foward to meeting the boy and taking him home to show the neighbours. A French student staying with them. That would give the street something to talk about for a while.

Susi's thoughts strayed briefly to Alan. Their row gave her a sad feeling inside, and she hadn't slept well for a couple of nights. But it was up to him to apologise. She hadn't started it. In a way, she hoped this student turned out to be dead good-looking, just to make Alan get really worried.

Crowds of people pushed their way past them, carrying cases labelled with foreign place names. They craned their necks for their visitor. He'd been told to look for them and Mrs. MacMahon held up a card with the words 'Pierre Lavalle' written on it in her best handwriting.

Suddenly, a boyish voice piped up behind them.

## SPOTTY

"Madame MacMeun?" it said.

Susi turned to find a small, dark-haired lad smiling at them. He was everything that she hadn't expected . . . plump, spotty, greasy-haired. You name it, he hadn't got it.

Disillusioned by her sample of French charm, she sat rather awkwardly next to him in the back of the car as they drove home. Her mother did most of the talking, experimenting with her holiday French, which made it even more embarrassing for her disappointed daughter.

"Hey, that must be him!" Tucker yelled as the car whizzed past. He was coming out of the newsagent's shop in Brooke Road with Tommy Watson.

"Wait 'til we tell Al," Tommy grinned.

Alan didn't believe them when they said he had no competition. That the guy had looked pretty revolting. He wanted to see for himself. But he didn't want to go rushing round to Susi's first thing, so he gave it a few days, then strolled past her house. No sign of life. He stopped at the end of the street. Maybe they were all out. He thought for a while then turned round and went slowly back again.

"Hi," he half-smiled when Susi answered the door. "Just came to say sorry," he mumbled, contemplating his feet.

"Accepted," she answered.

He tried to see past her into the narrow hall.

"Looking for something?" she asked.

"Like what?" He hated being caught out.

"Like Pierre, for instance? He arrived three days ago. We're taking him to the Odeon tonight."

"Oh, yeah?" Alan snorted, as his jealousy came flooding back. "Back row, is it?"

"What, with my mother there?" she asked. He looked knowingly at her. "You don't believe me, do you! Idiot!"

It was the signal for another argument to break out. Soon they were at it again, yelling and screaming at each other, until Susi's mum came to the door and told him to leave.

"I will not tolerate such behaviour on my doorstep," she said, showing him the gate. "Especially when we have a guest in the house!"

Susi watched Alan stomp off down the street, then went indoors to find Pierre sitting in the kitchen, cramming the last of his banana toffees down his throat. He ate an awful lot of sweets, she thought.

## SWINGS

Ten minutes later, she was walking down Sebastopol Road with him following her like a little puppy. Halfway along the street, there was a small patch of grass with some swings and a roundabout on it. There she saw Alan, sitting moping on a bench. He didn't see them. Not until Pierre made his move.

"Voici!" he shouted, pointing to the swings. Next thing Susi knew, he was on one, demanding a push. "Come on, Susi!" he urged.

Susi wanted the ground to open up and swallow her. She saw Alan watching now, trying not to smile.

So this was lover boy, he grinned to himself.

"*I'll* give you a shove, mate!" he shouted, heading for the swings. "'Course, you're not allowed on these, really. You're too old, understand?" Pierre didn't and carried on swinging.

Within a quarter of an hour, Pierre and Alan were mates, getting on really well and leaving Susi right out of it. It amused Alan to see how childish Pierre was—he still wanted to play dopey games! Alan wouldn't normally have been seen dead riding on the roundabout, but by playing along with him, he was putting one over on Susi who soon stormed off in a huff. Pierre could come home when he liked, as far as she was concerned!

That afternoon, Alan introduced Pierre to Tucker and Tommy.

"He's a nutter," he told them on the side, trusting that Pierre's English wouldn't be up to understanding what a nutter was, even if he overheard him. "Just you watch."

They did . . . as he accompanied them past the High Street market, touching things that he shouldn't touch and getting an earful from angry stallholders. Pierre giggled excitedly at some toy monkeys bobbing up and down on bits of elastic—and even bought one. Then he upset a couple of old ladies in nearby houses by running along the tops of their front garden walls, frightening their cats.

## KNACK

Next, they headed for the amusement arcade where he spent a bomb on one-armed bandits and games.

"Blimey, he's loaded," Tucker gasped, seeing the purseful of money that he had.

It didn't, however, take him long to get *un*loaded.

"Not like that," Tucker sighed, watching him press all the wrong buttons on the Casino Casablanca. "There's a knack to it. Here, lemme show ya!"

He edged Pierre out of the way and began playing the machine himself. Ten minutes later, Pierre had half his money back and seemed highly delighted. He treated them all to hamburger and chips.

After that, it was back to Tommy's place for international arm wrestling. England versus France. The French didn't stand a ghoster, being outnumbered three to one. Pierre's arm soon gave out on him and Alan made it 20-nil to loud cheers from the England supporters. That's when Mrs. Watson gave them all the boot from under her feet.

"You like football?" Pierre asked, pointing to a Hammers photograph in a neighbour's window. "I like!"

"Sorry, pal. None of us are all that keen!" Alan informed him.

Pierre seemed disappointed. It was one of his ambitions to see the famous Spurs playing at White Hart Lane, he told them.

"Go on. You take him, Al. He's your mate!" Tucker grinned, knowing the price of tickets.

"We will go?" Pierre pleaded, delighted that someone had been nominated.

Alan groaned. Why'd Tucker

have to go and open his big mouth? Now he'd just have to go and disappoint the kid again.

"I will buy the tickets!" came the startling offer.

Suddenly, it was a different ball game. They were all keen to go, but Al said he wouldn't dream of letting a good friend down . . .

* * * * *

The MacMahons were none too pleased with the way things had turned out. They were seeing hardly anything of their new lodger. He was always out with 'the boys'. Mrs. MacMahon had a word with him but for all the difference it made, she might as well have been speaking a different language. In Pierre's eyes, Alan and Co. could do no wrong.

"This Saturday," he enthused when he told Susi about the football match. "Against Manchester United!"

Left out in the cold again, she thought. He should be staying at Alan's place, not hers.

"Whose colours are they?" Alan asked when Pierre turned up wearing a green and black striped scarf.

## GAME

It turned out they were his school's, which didn't really surprise Alan much. What a wally!

"Come on, then, we're a bit late getting there," Alan urged, and they set off in the direction of the ground.

Several streets away, they met their first group of fans, a bunch of skinheads singing and chanting their way along. Better not mix it with that lot, Alan thought. Pierre had other ideas.

"Tottenham! Tottenham!" he shouted, in response to their chants of Uni-ted. It was all part of a game to him.

"Blimey," said Alan, turning white. "What'd you do that for?"

The shaven-headed lads in red and white were striding their way, their boots getting bigger with every step.

"Come on! Move!"

But it was too late. Pierre was surrounded. Brutality was a few seconds away. Alan watched, helplessly, from a hundred yards down the street. Then all hell broke loose as the skinheads got to work on Pierre. There was nothing for it but to go back and help him get away from them.

That night, Pierre returned home with his face cut and bruised, his anorak torn and his ticket money still in his pocket. It was the final straw for the MacMahons. They bathed his wounds, but first thing on Monday morning, he was sent home with a note, explaining the situation.

## PURPLE

There goes my trip to France, Susi thought. Not that she wanted to go now anyway. Not after meeting Pierre. Maybe he'd invite Alan instead.

* * * * *

"Good match, was it?" Tucker grinned, seeing the state of Al's face. One eye was almost closed. A dark purple patch just below it told its own story.

"Leave it out," Alan groaned. He didn't want to discuss football or Pierre. "That kid's a nutter. I told ya. Blimey, almost got me done in!"

"Well . . . don't look at us, mate! Not that you can all that well!" Tucker joked. "If you'd taken us with you, you'd have been all right!"

"Huh! *You* wouldn't, though!"

"Anyway, we're off down the market. Coming?" asked Tucker, moving towards Alan's gate.

"Nah, think I'll give it a rest," Alan frowned. "See you tonight maybe!" He gave a tired shrug and went inside. Tucker and Tommy wandered off, smiling at the state of their mate.

The house was empty. Mum was out shopping. Alan was on his own. He put a record on the deck and started listening to the second track. Susi had bought him the album for his last birthday . . . It had got halfway through when the phone rang. To his surprise, it *was* Susi.

"Pierre told me about Saturday," she explained. "Just calling to see if you're all right."

"Yeah, just a few bruises, nothing serious," he said, glad to know she still cared. "How's Pierre? Get back home to your house okay?"

"He's gone," she said. "Left this morning."

There was a one minute silence. Gone, eh, thought Alan. He wasn't sorry. With mates like him who needs enemies?

"On your tod again then, are you?" he asked. She told him she was. "Well then, fancy coming out tonight? Show you my scars!"

She laughed. What a flaming week it'd been. Talk about a French lesson . . .!

**THE END**

*"See you tonight maybe!"*

## ANNETTE FIRMAN
### (Nadia Chambers)

BIRTHDAY: 13th January, 1968 STAR SIGN: Capricorn
FAVOURITE FOOD: Chicken curry and chips
HOBBIES: Tap, ballet and modern dancing, singing and roller skating
PETS: Cat named Phaedra BROTHERS: 1 older, Karl SISTERS: 2 older, Kim and Tania
OTHER APPEARANCES: Parts in stage school shows, a TV advertisement for toasters, modelling for Marks and Spencer clothes

# OWN UP QUIZ!

# Who's a secret wally?

***What do you mean, you've no idea what a wally is? A wally is the kind of wet creep who always sits next to the Head in school photographs. The one person in the whole school who actually wears full school uniform and does every scrap of homework on time! But what you don't realise is that for every creep you can see, there are ten secret wallies lurking around, just waiting to do a good deed or two! Could you be one of 'em? Do our quiz and find out!***

***Then test all your friends to see how they get on with the questions. Who knows what you'll discover!***

**1.**
**Of course, you wouldn't be seen dead wearing your school uniform! But do you know where it is? Is it—**
a) Hanging in the wardrobe—right at the back, of course!?
b) Screwed up under the bed with a few ancient odd socks, *Grange Hill* magazines, etc.?
c) Hanging up right where you can see it? Er . . . yes, you do try it on sometimes—but only for a giggle. Well, you secretly like to look smart and efficient!

**2.**
**You're on your way home from school on the crowded bus one night when you spot 'Miss' doing a dodgy balancing act with a couple of shopping bags. Do you—**
a) Politely offer her your seat?
b) Hide behind your comic so she doesn't see you?
c) Trip her up as you get off!?

**3.**
**It's your school's sports day. You know for a fact that the Head and all the parents are going to be there, watching you do your stuff! Are you more likely to—**
a) Bunk off so you don't have to go through with it?
b) Pretend you've sprained your ankle—you'd rather sit and watch!?
c) Stay up all night, ironing your sports kit—you'd hate to let the school down!

**4.**
**If your house caught fire, the first thing you'd grab under your arm to save would be—**
a) Your mum?
b) Your maths homework?
c) Your record collection?

**5.**
**Yes, it's time for that annual disaster—the school play! You know for a fact that the drama teacher is out talent spotting! Would you—**
a) Keep as far away from the stage as possible?
b) Hang around in corridors till someone notices your—er—star potential!?
c) Offer to help backstage?

**6.**
**You find the answers to an important exam lying in the corridor. It's the one you're taking the very next morning! Do you—**
a) Run straight to the Head's office with your find—without so much as a teeny weeny glance?
b) Take a quick peep but hand them back to a teacher?
c) Sell copies to all your friends at ten pence a time?

SCORE

| | a | b | c |
|---|---|---|---|
| 1 | 5 | 10 | 0 |
| 2 | 0 | 5 | 10 |
| 3 | 10 | 5 | 0 |
| 4 | 5 | 0 | 10 |
| 5 | 10 | 0 | 5 |
| 6 | 0 | 5 | 10 |

WELL? ARE YOU A BIG WET? OWN UP!

0-15: Good golly, what a wally! What's worse, you don't hide it all that well, either! Get up off the floor right now and stop being such a crawler! There's nothing wrong with mucking about with your mates sometimes, you know!

If you carry on being such a drip, they'll wash their hands of you!

20-40: Not bad! You like to be helpful and do your best, and you don't mind who knows it—but you're not quite creepy enough to make it as a wally! But then, you don't really want to be one, do you?

If you begin starching your school tie though, it's time to watch out!

45-60: No-one could call you a wally in a million years! They wouldn't get away with it, for a start—you're just too tough! But wouldn't you like to be a wally, just once in a while? After all, there's one good thing about 'em—they're never in trouble with teachers!

They may be famous, but they'll never forget their...

# SPECIAL SCHOOL FRIENDS

## Girl trouble for Duran Duran...

It was being spurned by an old school-mate—a girl in fact—that led Simon Le Bon into the music business, and on to eventual success as lead singer with Duran Duran.

### DETERMINED

"This girl—who shall remain nameless—just laughed when I told her I'd like to be a pop star. I became determined to prove that I could make the grade, so now I'm having the last laugh! In a way, I'm glad she didn't believe me. Maybe I'd never have got on without that push."

And further proof that the boys in Duran Duran are actually as friendly as they look when they appear on TV, bass-man John Taylor informed us that his best mate at school was none other than Nick Rhodes, who now plays keyboards in this chart-topping band.

## Bowie bunked off!

Superstar David Bowie remembers his schooldays very well, and although he wasn't too keen on the regular lessons, he managed to grin and bear it! That was all thanks to having a good friend on hand in the shape of the now equally famous Peter Frampton. They had quite a bit in common.

### LOVE OF MUSIC

"Peter and I were both local lads," David says, "living, going to school in, and generally hanging around in the Beckenham area of Kent. I can't really say that it was our mutual love of music that brought us together—we were just mates like anyone else. We did all the normal things like bunking off class together and having the odd sly fag when no-one was looking."

### AMERICAN VISITS

And does David see much of his old friend these days?

"I try to keep in touch," he says, "and I look Peter up whenever I'm in the States—which is actually quite often! We like each other's company"

STAR memories

# Polecats apart

"Actually, it wasn't so easy making friends at school," recalls Tim Worman, lead singer with rockabilly four-piece, The Polecats. "What with being interested in rockabilly music, and all.

**PUNK EXPLOSION**

"Trouble was, when the band and I were at senior school, it was the middle of the punk explosion. While everyone else would be waffling on about The Sex Pistols or The Damned, all we really wanted to talk about were obscure American artists from the 1950s that no one had ever heard of! It was crazy."

Along came drummer Phil, though, and through him Tim and guitar-player Boz became firm friends and went on to form the band.

But how did it come about? Where did they all get together to create their own sound?

**FORCED TO MOVE**

"Well, you could say that my school career was a bit, er, chequered," admits Phil, "and I was forced to move on from a place called Moat Mount school—where I'd been mates with Boz—to Orange Hill school which is where I met Tim. When I realised that we were all into exactly the same things, our very close friendship really took off in a big way."

And shows no signs of touching down, either!

# Japan and the bullies

"We do have a rather pretty-boy image, I suppose," says Japan's lead singer David Sylvian, "and a lot of people think that it's all just a gimmick. But it isn't—we've always looked this way, more or less, and it was our common obsession with fashion, make-up and just looking good that brought us all together in the first place. It also keeps us firm friends to this day!"

**MORAL SUPPORT**

And going back to David's mention of how the band "came together in the first place", they're another of today's successful groups who were firm school-mates first and talented pop stars second. Seems exercise books and guitars *do* mix!

"It was at senior school that we met," recalls David, "and we used to give each other a lot of moral support. Sometimes that wasn't enough however—real protection was needed! From a gang of real thugs.

"When the bully-boys were looking for someone to use as a punch bag, we tended to be on the top of their list. So we decided to always move around as a group just for our own safety, and the idea sort of spilled over into our adult lives and we stayed together as Japan".

And, as you don't really need us to tell you, very successfully!

# Adam's years of torture

Main Ant-man Adam had a rather unusual friend when he was at school—his art teacher!

"That's right," says Adam, "I was at a school called St. Marylebone's Grammar, and wasn't enjoying it one little bit.

**NON-STOP EXAMS**

"All my pals had gone to the local comprehensive, and I would have loved to have gone with them so as not to have broken up the gang."

But, as he sadly recalls, Adam was just a bit too clever for his own good and wound up in the grammar school which was torture for him—a non-stop round of exams, revision, and then more exams. All that work was a heavy weight to carry.

**SO CHUMMY**

"All I ever wanted to do was art," says Adam, "and my teacher realised it. He could see that I had talent, and he really encouraged me. He was the nearest thing to a friend I ever had in that place, and though you can't exactly get on first name terms with one of your teachers when you're only fifteen or sixteen, he was so chummy that I don't think he'd really have minded if I had stopped calling him 'Sir'."

But now that Adam's at the top of the tree, does he ever look up his old teacher and talk over old times? Do they discuss videos and special costumes? Adam's new look and his make-up designs?

"I'd love to," says Adam, "but sadly he died of pleurisy just when I was about to take my A-levels. I felt the loss as much as I would if he'd been a member of my own family! I'll never forget him . . ."

"We're sure you won't, Adam.

# Stray Cats in street fights!

"Friends?" asks Brian Setzer, leader of those American rebel rockers, The Stray Cats. "Yeah—you really needed your friends back there on the streets of New York. It can get tough at times—there are a lot of street gangs just hanging around waiting for the chance to lay some muscle on you.

**FAIR SHARE**

"And seeing as how I ain't exactly Mr. Universe, I've had my fair share of trouble!"

But Brian has also found that whenever he's been in a tight spot, he's been able to rely on his old school-friends, Lee Rocker and Slim Jim Phantom—the dynamic duo who lay down the rhythm parts of The Stray Cats' sound.

**MORE FIGHTS**

"They've pulled me out of more fights than I care to remember," says Brian, "but then—that's what friends are for, ain't it?"

# LOSER TAKES ALL

Later . . .
I HEAR YOU'RE THE NEW DUNCAN GOODHEW OF THE THIRD YEAR!
LEAVE OFF! I'M HANGING ON TO ALL MY BLINKIN' HAIR!
BLIMEY! MY BIKE – IT'S BEEN WRECKED!
WHAT MORON WOULD DO A THING LIKE THAT?
WALKING HOME TONIGHT, ARE YA, ORPINGTON?
STEBSON! I MIGHT HAVE GUESSED!
YOU'VE BEEN AT MY BIKE, HAVEN'T YOU!
DUANE! DON'T!
SAYS WHO?
SAYS ME!
OH, YEAH? YOU GOING TO DO SOMETHING ABOUT IT, THEN?
YEAH, I AM!
PACK IT IN, DUANE! HE'S JUST LOOKING FOR A FIGHT!
REPORT IT TOMORROW, IF YOU'RE SURE IT WAS HIM!
NO WAY! I'LL FIGHT MY OWN BATTLES!
THINK YOURSELF LUCKY, ORPINGTON!
Next day . . .
HID BEHIND CLAIRE SCOTT, DID YA?
LEAVE IT OUT!
DRRINGGG!!
I'D HAVE HAD HIM, IF SHE HADN'T STOPPED ME! AND HE KNOWS IT!
OH, YEAH? GOOD JOB HE ISN'T LISTENING!
ALL DONE YOUR HOMEWORK, I HOPE!
OF COURSE, SIR!

But . . .
I MUST'VE LEFT MY BOOK AT HOME, SIR! I DID DO IT, HONEST!
EXCUSES, ORPINGTON!
UNLIKE YOU, I HAVEN'T GOT WATER ON THE BRAIN! ANY MORE OF THIS AND I'LL HAVE YOU WITHDRAWN FROM THE SWIMMING GALA!
I DID PUT IT IN MY BAG — I KNOW I DID!
Then . . .
WHERE HAVE YOU BEEN, POGO? I LOOKED EVERYWHERE!
HEY, WHAT HAPPENED?
WHAT DO YOU THINK? STEBSON!
I CAUGHT HIM STUFFING YOUR HOME-WORK BOOK DOWN THE BOG! I TOLD YOU HE'S MAD!
ALL THIS OVER A FLAMING RACE?
IT'S MORE THAN THAT TO HIM!
RIGHT! HE'S ASKED FOR IT! I'LL HIT HIM WHERE IT HURTS MOST!
So, on gala day . . .
STILL RECKON ON WINNING, ORPINGTON?
SAVE YOUR BREATH, STEBSON! YOU'LL NEED IT FOR BLOWING UP YOUR WATER-WINGS!
THUMP!
THINK YOU'RE SMART? SEE HOW WELL YOU CAN SWIM WITH ONE ARM!
AAAGH!
I SAW THAT, STEBSON! HOW'D YOU LIKE TO SPEND THE AFTERNOON BACK AT SCHOOL?
HEH! THAT'LL TEACH HIM!

THAT PUT STEBSON IN HIS PLACE!
HMPH! NOTHING GETS THROUGH TO THAT THICK-HEAD!
HEY, YOU KNOW YOU AREN'T SUPPOSED TO EAT ANYTHING BEFORE YOU GO SWIMMING!
LEAVE OFF! I'M STARVING!
FIRST, CATHY SMITH . . . SECOND, LINDSEY PETERS!
HOORAAAY!
NEXT RACE, THE THIRD YEAR BOYS' FREE-STYLE!
COME ON, DUANE!
YOU GOTTA WIN IT, DUANE!
BANG!!
GO! GO! GO!
RIGHT, STEBSON! THIS IS IT!
AND STRAIGHT AWAY, DUANE ORPINGTON TAKES THE LEAD!
HOORAAAY!
ORPINGTON TURNS FIRST, TEN YARDS CLEAR!
SPLADOOSH!
SURELY NO-ONE CAN CATCH HIM NOW!
GOTTA KEEP GOING! GOTTA SMASH HIM INTO THE GROUND!
Suddenly . . .
I'M SINKING . . . I CAN'T . . . GULP!
AAAGH!!
HELP!
FASTER! FASTER!
POGO! HE'S IN TROUBLE!

AAAGH! SPLUTTER!
HANG ON!
SPLASH!
OOOH! GURGLE!
BLIMEY, STOP STRUGGLING!
YOU DID WELL THERE, LAD! HAD THE RACE IN YOUR POCKET, TOO!
IS HE OKAY?
LUCKY YOU DUCKED OUT THERE, ORPINGTON! KNEW WHAT WAS GOOD FOR YOU, EH!
GET OUT OF MY SIGHT, STEBSON! YOU MAKE MY STOMACH TURN!
SIR??
A few days later . . .
DID YOU A FAVOUR THERE! SAVED YOU FROM GRIPPER! BEST BIT OF ACTING I'VE EVER DONE!
OH, YEAH? DELIBERATE, WAS IT?
LIKE HELL!
'COURSE IT WAS! I KNEW WHAT'D HAPPEN IF YOU BEAT HIM!
HEY, YOU! YOU OWE ME A QUID!
WHAT?
HAVEN'T GOT A QUID, GRIPPER! ANY-WAY . . . OOW! LEGGO!
WELL, YOU'D BETTER FIND IT THEN!
LAY OFF HIM!
HEH, HEH! FANCY PRETENDING TO DROWN AND GIVING UP A QUID, POGO! WHAT A MATE!
OH, SHURRUP!
THE END

# Lee's not just a great actor, he's... A BRIGHT SPARK!

## WITH A CHEEKY GRIN AND WICKED WINK

Some people have all the luck. And Lee Sparke seems to be one of them! Playing the part of Jonah in *Grange Hill* came easily to him, because he "just sort of fell into acting."

When Lee was a tot, he had no great ambition to get into show business—or even to play a leading part in a popular TV serial. But then at only six years old, how many kids do know what they want to do? That was the age Lee started his career, though! His qualifications? Being cheeky!

A mop of blond hair and great dimples were little Lee's only assets. But they were enough!

## HE'D WORK FOR BURGERS – NOT PEANUTS!

"Yes, it's true," he remembers. "My cousin just happened to be looking through a newspaper one day when she noticed an advertisement placed by an agency looking for cheeky boys.

"Well, I went along and I must have looked the part because I got accepted straight away."

Since then, Lee's never looked back. He's done countless commercials—"So many I don't remember them all—but I do remember enjoying muching my way through the McDonald's one!"

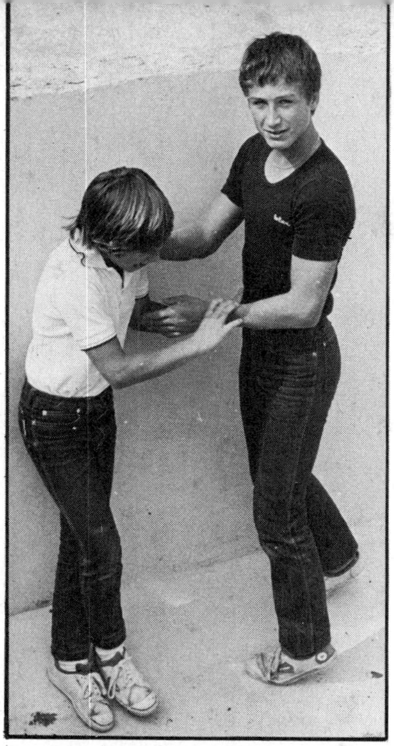

## THE SAME KIND OF GUY AS TUCKER

He's worked on TV serials like *Thomas and Sarah*—and, of course, *Grange Hill.*

"I was over the moon when I heard I'd been picked for *Grange Hill.* It was touch and go. Originally, they'd chosen someone else for my part. Luckily, however, somewhere along the line they'd realised he wasn't quite suitable.

"It was a really big thing to happen to my life—probably one of the biggest. And I was—and still am—really excited. I like playing Jonah. I'm a bit of a Tucker Jenkins sort, I suppose.

"My mates take the mickey at school (he goes to an ordinary non-stage school near his home in South Woodford) and call me Jonah, but I don't mind."

## LOTS OF FIGHTS IN THE FAMILY

"There've been some funny things happen during filming, like the time I couldn't get my lines right. I had a real mouthful to deliver. Everyone ended up in fits—including me. Another time we were on location in Chessington Zoo. Now that was fun because we were allowed to wander round in between filming! It was a special treat for the whole cast."

Professional life aside, Lee leads an ordinary family life. "I row with my older brother, Dane, a lot. I suppose we sort of get on. But he hits me—so I hit him back. I don't just stand there!"

## SWIMMING'S HIS SPECIAL HOBBY

His mum's very proud of Lee, and always offers loads of encouragement, but doesn't help with his lines. "Probably because I've never asked her," says Lee. "I learn them through rehearsing so much anyway.

"My whole family's pleased for me," says Lee. "But they make sure I keep up with my schoolwork. And that can get a bit difficult. Except when I'm doing my two favourite subjects—history and geography. I don't mind working hard at those. . . "

In his spare (if any) time, he likes to roller skate—"I'm quite good, I can go backwards!"—and swim. Water is the great love of his life. So much so, that the family had a pool built in their back garden.

"I helped to dig it out," he grins. "It's smashing 'cos it's heated. Means I can swim all year round, though it does get a bit cold when there's snow on the ground." Lee used to like getting round on his bike as well, but since our photos of him were taken, the bike no longer exists!

## PLEASE SAY HELLO WHEN YOU SEE HIM!

"Put it like this," he confides. "We parted company. It sort of fell apart! Near the end, there was only the rust holding it together. The whole frame crumbled to a brown dust! Then the wheels fell off . . ."

He also likes just sitting around and dreaming of the time when fans will rush up to him in the street. "I shan't mind at all," he says. "Not like some actors. In fact, I'm quite looking forward to it!"

THE GRANGE HILL INTERVIEW

They say he's in a special class of his own, and if you want to know why, come with us and . . .

## Learnalong-a-Buster!

# DOUG from WOODBERRY DOWN!

**Woodberry Down comprehensive school in North London closed down recently. Douglas Trendle, also known as Buster Bloodvessel, sometimes known as Fatty, and always leader with chart-toppers Bad Manners—thinks he knows why.**

"They knew they'd never turn out anyone as famous as me again," he says with a grin, "so they thought they might as well close down rather than begin to try!"

But in a more serious mood, Doug admits that he actually enjoyed his schooldays and is quite sad that the old place is no more.

"I made some good friends at Woodberry Down," he recalls. "In fact, me and most of the band were in the same year. I think that the friends you make at school are the best kind—and so far I haven't been proved wrong!"

### "I GAVE UP"

Making friends was never that hard for Dougie Trendle—all his school reports show he was always a lively and popular pupil, even if he sometimes had "spasms of silly behaviour" and let "his love of fun prevent him from success in his work"!

But although life at the comprehensive was generally pleasant, Doug's early days at primary school were sometimes a little fraught.

"It was when I was seven years old that most of the trouble began," he remembers. "For a start, I was involved in a car crash that kept me off school for a long time. When I eventually returned, I found that all my mates were streets ahead of me when it came to reading and writing."

"What do you think I did?" he demands. "I gave up, of course! Well, you do when you're only little. After a while it seems easiest not to bother."

### "THE KIDS FOUND OUT"

But, as he found out, that attitude generally gets you nowhere fast.

"At Woodberry Down," he says, "one of my favourite subjects was drama. I even had ambitions of being an actor at one time. But, not being too hot on the old reading and that, I had a lot of trouble learning and remembering my lines!

"The second thing that made my days at primary school memorable was that I found out that I was adopted. I learned, although I don't think I was supposed to, that the lady I'd always called Mum wasn't my real mum at all. When the kids at school found out they gave me a lot of stick. One boy in particular used to call me some dreadful names.

"Then one day I threatened to knock his block off. After that, he started being nice to me and so did all the other kids—they started treating me as if I was something special, and I started to believe I was, too!

"I think it was that belief in myself that helped me to get on!"

Doug's teachers at Woodberry Down weren't exactly slack when it came to encouragement, either.

A few of Doug's mates had banded together to form a group which they called Snacks At The Bar.

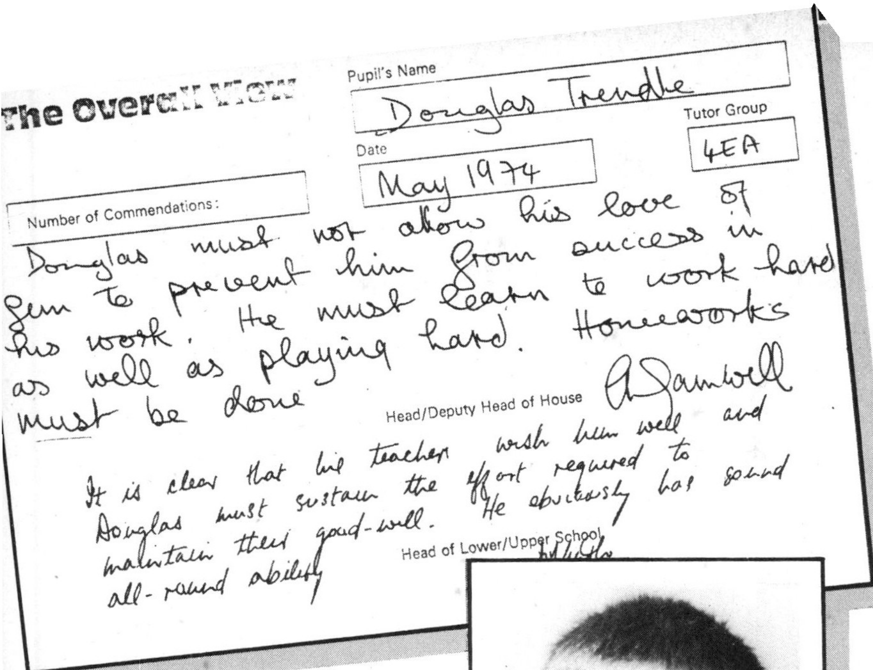

The Overall View

Pupil's Name: Douglas Trendle

Tutor Group: 4EA

Date: May 1974

Number of Commendations:

Douglas must not allow his love of fun to prevent him from success in his work. He must learn to work hard as well as playing hard. Homeworks must be done

A Gambell

Head/Deputy Head of House

It is clear that his teachers wish him well and Douglas must sustain the effort required to maintain their good-will. He obviously has sound all-round ability

Head of Lower/Upper School

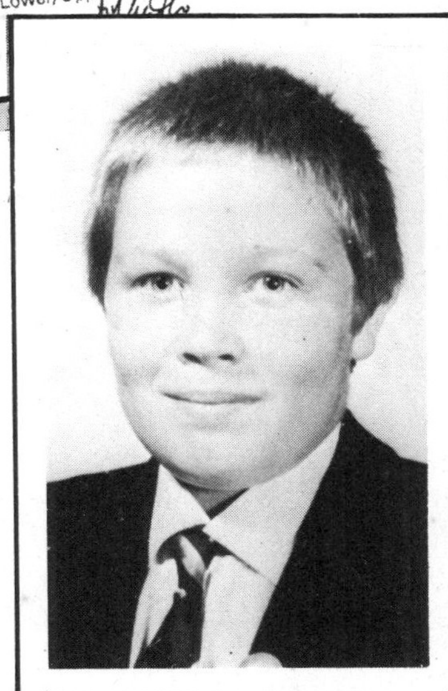

When they heard the fledgling Bad Manners fooling around, trying to get songs together, the teachers urged them to take music more seriously.

"So we did," says Doug, "and even gave impromptu concerts in the assembly hall. Of course, we were a bit ragged in those days—some of our critics still think we are!—but it was all good practice, and it really does help to know that there are people on your side!"

## "ALL A BIT OF FUN"

But in spite of all this moral support, did Doug and the boys ever really think that they'd become the stars that they are today? Known by nearly all music fans?

"No," says Doug, "not really. Like I said, it was all a bit of fun. I think perhaps the only sign that my life *was* going to change was that I started to put on weight.

"See, I was really skinny up until I was abut nine or ten, but after that—which was just about the time I started at Woodberry Down—the pounds began to pile on. And they haven't stopped!"

## "I WAS EASILY BORED"

As Doug's love of music and performing grew, his interest in his academic life waned.

"I didn't mind going along to the lessons," he admits, "but I was easily bored, and when it came to homework—very little of that got done!"

Doug came up with some good excuses as to why not, but his most common reason was that he'd lost his homework diary.

All together now—aaah!

"Well, actually, that's more or less how my teachers used to react," says Doug with a grin. "I was always thought of as 'a bit slap-dash in looking after belongings'."

During one year, Doug was reported for having done no homework at all in physics!

But apart from a rather lazy attitude when it came to the hard part of school life, Doug was very loyal to Woodberry Down, He was a ferociously keen member of the rugby team, and always made sure that he turned up for the matches.

So far, Doug's school career has seemed to be pretty much like anyone else's—it had its ups and downs, but on the whole it wasn't too dreadful.

But then came the biggest disappointment of young Doug's life.

## "YOU CAN LAUGH"

Stand by with your Kleenex, because this is going to break you up.

We're ready—so care to tell us about it, Doug?

"Yes," he sighs, "my biggest ever disappointment was . . . not getting the part of Mother Goose in the school play! Oh, you can laugh—but it meant a lot to me, that part. See, I always liked to be in the limelight, and having the starring role wherever possible. Most times I managed it. But on this occasion I lost out—and to my arch rival, too!"

Doug did get a role in the play, though—as Bert, one of the villains of the piece.

But it wasn't the same

Still, Dougie kept on smiling, and fooling around as much as ever.

## "WE CHANGED THE NAME"

"Oh, I never stopped doing that," he laughs. "I always loved a good laugh. That was part of the reason for forming Bad Manners—we just wanted to have some fun. If we got paid for it into the bargain—all the better!"

But when Doug and his mates finally left Woodberry Down, the money didn't start coming in right away.

"I was a navvy for a while," says Doug, "and I'd play with the band in the evening. At that time we were called Stoop Solo And The Street Starchers—but no-one could remember that, so we changed the name to Bad Manners—and the rest you know."

And how do your old school friends—or teachers—react to you now that you're an international success?

## "JUST A FASHION"

"They love it!" says Doug. "I still see some of the teachers and a few of the blokes from the old school, and really they're well pleased that we've gone ahead and made a go of something that they'd never have even thought of doing."

Even in spite of some of the bad publicity you've had? After all, it hasn't been all sweetness and light, has it?

"I suppose you're referring to all the skinhead trouble that we had in the early days," muses Doug. "Well, just 'cos some of us look like skinheads, it doesn't mean that we are going to rush out and stomp on people.

"It's just a fashion that goes with the music, and if it attracts some of the heavier skinheads to our gigs, then that's just unfortunate. We make it clear that violence isn't welcome, but you can't really stop anyone coming into a show, can you?"

Buster sighs, then adds: "All you can really do is just hope that people forget themselves and have a good time. After all, that's what Bad Manners is all about!"

# Very tricky Grange Hill quiz

# AN EXAM FOR A FAN!

**Can you remember the facts from series five? We tested you on your knowledge of other episodes in the 1982 annual—so see how you do here.**

**1. Who locked himself in the toilets one day?**
a) Tucker Jenkins.
b) Booga.
c) Roland.

**2. Someone managed to get him out. Who was it?**
a) Alan.
b) Jonah.
c) Doyle.

**3. How did he do this?**
a) By throwing a stink bomb through the window.
b) By forcing the door open with a metal bar.
c) By pretending the school was on fire.

**4. Which boy did Annette get into trouble at the zoo?**
a) Carrots.
b) Nigel.
c) Turnip.

**5. How did she make him do something wrong? And what was it?**
a) She pretended she wanted a cold drink and got him to steal one.
b) She climbed onto the dinosaur and said she couldn't get down, so he had to climb up too.
c) She told him it was okay to feed the giraffes even though a sign said it was wrong.

**6. What were Pogo's main money-making schemes?**
a) Hiring out text books and selling answers to exam papers.
b) Forging homework and end-of-term reports for other pupils.
c) Taking bets on how many times the school football team would score in a term and selling Coke at half-time.

**7. Which teacher did Claire write about in her diary?**
a) Mr. Sutcliffe.
b) Mr. Hopwood.
c) Mr. Baxter.

**8. Jonah, Zammo, Fay, Roland, Belinda and Annette started in which form?**
a) G1.
b) E1.
c) N1.

**9. What was the new school subject that parents objected to?**
a) Rugby.
b) Computer studies.
c) Sex education.

**10. A new teacher joined *Grange Hill*. Do you know his name and main subjects?**
a) Stuffy Smith—geography and history.
b) Growler Morgan—maths and physics.
c) Scruffy McGuffy—English and drama.

**11. What happened to Roland to keep him away from school?**
a) His parents moved house and he couldn't travel so far.
b) He got run over and went to hospital.
c) He caught chicken pox and then measles.

**12. Who was Jonah and Zammo's form teacher?**
a) Miss Mooney.
b) Miss Hartford.
c) Miss McDonald.

**13. What did pupils have to collect for the *Grange Hill* sponsorship scheme?**
a) Stamps.
b) Egg boxes.
c) Sweet wrappers.

## MARKING TIME

*The correct answers are . . .*
*1-c, 2-b, 3-a, 4-a, 5-b, 6-a, 7-b, 8-c, 9-c, 10-c, 11-b, 12-a, 13-c, 14-b, 15-c, 16-a.*

*You get two points for each!*

*0-8: Pathetic! Stand in the corner with a paper bag over your head and repeat, "I must not watch* Grange Hill *and try to do my homework and eat my tea at the same time" until you really believe what you're saying! Okay? Okay!*

*10-20: Huh! Half-hearted about the best children's programme the world's ever seen, eh? Shame on you!*

*22-32: Well, you certainly know your stuff! If you got full marks in the 40 Questions quiz in the last* Grange Hill *annual, then you deserve a special certificate or something. Maybe a medal!*

**14. Who found himself in a sticky situation over badges?**
a) Roland.
b) Jonah.
c) Zammo.

**15. And who was it who sneaked?**
a) Doyle.
b) Alan Humphries.
c) Gripper Stebson.

**16. Whose musical instrument went missing?**
a) Belinda's.
b) Annette's.
c) Fay's.

# BEHIND THE BIKE~SHEDS!

# THE ODDS ARE AGAINST YOU!

**What would you do if someone gave you fifty quid? Spend it? Save it? Or do what Mick did? Chuck it all down the drain!**

His dad had given him the money for his birthday, to buy a second-hand bike. He'd have had second thoughts if he'd known what his son was intending to do with it that night.

Because Mick caught a train to the centre of town and by eleven o'clock—just a few hours later—he'd blown the lot in an amusement arcade.

### FURIOUS

He made up some lie to his dad about not finding the right bike, said he'd save the money instead, and his dad saw no reason not to believe him. It wasn't until a few weeks later—when money started disappearing from his wallet, that he began to suspect the truth.

Mick's dad didn't suspect him of being a full-blown gambler and thief, though. But that's just what he was fast turning into. Because that night up in town, Mick had well and truly caught the bug. It didn't worry him one bit that he'd spent all his birthday money. All that worried him was getting more money to gamble again. And Mick didn't find that too difficult.

**Take a chance on gambling—and you take an even bigger chance of ruining your life. A game can become a very big problem . . .**

At first he skipped school lunches to save the money, but when that wasn't enough, he 'borrowed' from his mum's purse. Trouble was, he never quite got round to putting it back. When things really got out of hand, he stole large sums of money from his dad.

And that didn't go unnoticed. His dad was furious. Threatened to turn him into the police, the lot, if he didn't stop. But Mick couldn't.

And when, a few months or so later he left school, Mick went onto bigger and 'better' things. The dogs and horses. He hung round the bookies most of his spare time, and as the stakes got higher, the more he stole—this time from his employers. As a direct result of this—just a short time from his first bet at school—he went to Borstal.

*A game of cards is harmless enough, isn't it?*

And if you reckon Mick's story is all a load of rubbish, made up to frighten you, you're wrong. Mick is a real person. And what's even more frightening—it could happen to you.

### STATUS

Because Mick's 'life of crime' started off behind the bike-sheds one lunch hour over a game of cards with the odds just five or ten pence a go. It probably happens at your school, too. And it's not too disastrous losing a couple of pence.

For some kids however, gambling becomes a kind of status thing. They want to drop out of a game but daren't because of the mickey-taking.

Besides, the day someone wins, they feel on top of the world. They forget the days they went without lunch to pay their debts. Maybe they celebrate by going along to the chippie for a treat . . .

And that's where they spend all their money again. Not on a double helping of fish, but on the fruit machines and Space Invaders.

One-armed bandits and space machines are a lot of fun, but only when you can keep them in perspective. When you get like Mick and can't keep away from them, you've got a problem.

The law says you're not allowed in bookmakers' shops until you're 18. But the law on fruit machines and electronic games is not quite so clear.

### DANGERS

Amusement arcades are a slightly different matter as well. The owners can make up their own age limit. And the police only have the power to act if, for example, the place is packed night after night with 'young punters'. Then they can have the arcade's licence removed. But it doesn't happen often enough.

Any sort of gambling's a fool's game, so don't start it. If you already have, try very hard to stop. And if you must hang round machines, keep away from the amusement arcades up town. The kind of people they attract—as well as the more obvious dangers of falling into the gambler's trap—should be avoided. Believe it!

# A REAL-LIFE NIGHTMARE

***Susi Hush—Producer of** Grange Hill **—takes you behind the scenes and tells you about her very special job . . .***

**There's never a dull moment when you're the Producer of a programme like *Grange Hill*, and that's the way Susi likes it. She's responsible for everything and everybody. And if that sounds like your idea of a nightmare, Susi readily admits that there are quite a few problems.**

Like, for example, the times when script writers don't stick to the deadlines!

Phil Redmond, the creator of *Grange Hill,* writes out all the storylines, but it's up to Susi to commission the actual scripts.

"And when they're late, it causes terrible problems," she admits. "It really does put everybody out.

"Not only that, sometimes the scripts still need rewriting when they arrive, so then we're all back to square one again!"

### DISCUSS

At the time we spoke to Susi, she was using four writers—two men and two women—who all have to be very tightly briefed. For Susi is also responsible for the continuity of the series.

"For example," she explained, "I have to watch the characters very carefully. If one writer writes an installment with an actor doing something very specific—like playing the role of a trouble-maker, I can't have another writer showing the same actor as an absolute angel in the very next episode. So, obviously, it's very important that we all keep in close contact and discuss things carefully.

"Some inexperienced writers' scripts use too many sets as well, which we just couldn't fit into one programme.

"I have to guide them and advise them on limitations too, or else they'd go really mad with lavish locations costing thousands of pounds. Believe me, the *Grange Hill* budget really does have to be watched carefully. It would be disastrous if all the money went on one episode due to an overenthusiastic script. I have to even it out over a whole series."

Susi has to stick to the *Grange Hill* school rules, too.

"What appears on the screen is as important as what's being said. We can't make any slips. I normally hang around during filming, and I remember one scene which was meant to be taking place around the bike-sheds during the lunch hour. I had to quickly call it to a halt. I'd suddenly remembered that the bike-sheds were supposed to be out of bounds!

"Another school rule bans the wearing of jewellery, so I have to watch out to make sure rings and bracelets aren't being worn by some of the girls."

Relationships between the staff and the pupils need to be closely scrutinised too—particularly on the emotional side.

And it can all, as Susi confesses, be very frustrating. "But it's also a smashing feeling having all the responsibility and knowing absolutely everything about the programme that there is to know—even if it is a bit hair-raising at times."

### FREELANCE

Susi did all the auditions for the new class in the fifth series as well—and that brought along its share of headaches, too.

"We saw hundreds and hundreds of children—and went to lots of different stage schools. A lot of the children initially chosen were good for just one particular part of the script—but I was looking for good all-rounders, so I had to be ruthless. And then with the licensing laws only allowing child actors to work so many hours, lots of juggling had to go on to work out when—and if—they could be used. It got quite complicated, but we finally made it and the new class was chosen."

Susi is, in fact, a freelance producer which means that she can work for ITV as well as the BBC. And her career to date has included work on *Crown Court, Girl Talk, Nanny Knows Best* and *Coronation Street*—which she loved. Even though, as she owns up, she did make one huge mistake.

### ERRORS

"I decided to take all of the leading female members of the cast to Majorca for a story—and, quite coincidentally, I chose a female writer to script the whole thing.

"As it turned out, the idea was a huge success, but when we got back to England, I was greeted by a very stony reception. All the men involved with *Coronation Street* were furious and accused me of being a female chauvinist! I could see their point, but up until then I hadn't even thought about that problem!"

Other disasters which meant snap decisions for Susi were when a lot of the cast were ill all together—and the sudden death of a key actor.

"I really learnt to think fast. I made mistakes of course, but I think you can only really learn through your errors anyway."

And it's a lesson Susi's learnt well. For if there are any errors in *Grange Hill,* they're sorted out a long time before they reach the televisions in our homes.

Sifting out faults—and a thousand and one other things—is all part of being a Producer . . .

*A look at why a visit to the fleapit costs a fortune!*

# SEEN ANY GOOD FILMS LATELY?

**When was the last time you went to the cinema? Was the film you saw a *U, A, AA* or *X* certificate? It's not likely to have been an X certificate film as you have to be eighteen or over to get into those—unless you lied about your age, of course!**

But what about the other categories of film laid down by the British Board of Film Censors? You will have already discovered that you can get into a cinema showing a U certificate film however young you are, and that the same is really true of A certificate films. The difference is that your parents are warned that A films contain some "adult" scenes which they may not wish you to see.

### WHO AGREES WITH FILM CENSORSHIP?

Lastly, AA certificates are given to films that the Censor has decided are unsuitable for anyone under 14. One cinema manager admitted that he often uses his own judgement when young people, who are obviously under-age are trying to get into a film considered unsuitable for them.

"If the film in question is very violent or deals with drug-taking, I'll turn them away," he said. But he did admit to letting in under-age people to films he personally thought were not particularly harmful.

Do you agree with film censorship? If you were the Censor, what kind of films would you stop young people from seeing? Write and tell us!

### CINEMAS ARE EXPENSIVE PLACES TO RUN

But getting into the film of your choice is not the only problem you have to face today. The full price for a cinema ticket is now well over two pounds and the reduced rate (for those under 14) is around half price. Not exactly a cheap night out, is it?

Most of the larger companies—ABC, Odeon, Classic, Star, etc—try to keep their prices in line with each other, but some cinemas outside London are cheaper. On the other hand, there's rarely any reduced rate for youngsters in London's West End.

But why does it cost so much to go to the cinema now? One reason is that cinemas are expensive places to heat and look after. A cinema's gas bill for three months can be as much as £7,000 or more. You have to sell a lot of tickets to get that back!

The main trouble though, is that we don't go to the cinema as often as we did in the past, since most films are now shown on television sooner or later. An awful lot of people feel it's worth waiting until they can watch the film in the comfort and privacy of their own homes. So with fewer seats being sold, prices must go up. Of course, you could argue that cinemas might sell more tickets if they were cheaper, but you'd have to argue that one out with the big companies that own them. It's a vicious circle.

Do you think you get your money's worth when you go to the cinema? Put your thoughts on paper and send them in.

One way of getting into a film without paying is to become a cinema usherette. You can apply for these jobs when you are sixteen years old. Full-time usherettes are paid a reasonable wage per week, but those working less than twenty hours a week get an hourly rate.

A cinema usherette working in London explained that the main disadvantage of the job is that she is working when other people are enjoying themselves. She also sometimes has to deal with difficult or rowdy customers. Maybe you're one of them . . .

### HAVE YOU EVER BEEN THROWN OUT?

Have you ever been thrown out of a cinema for noisy behaviour? It's not an offence to make a noise in a public place, but it is an offence to cause a disturbance. If the manager of a cinema thinks you're stopping other people in the cinema from enjoying the film, he can take action.

The film industry is certainly going through very difficult times, but perhaps cinema managers or owners could do more to attract people to cinemas. What improvements would you like to see in your local cinema? Let's hear your views!

# The GRANGE HILL

## January

| | | | | | |
|---|---|---|---|---|---|
| Su | | 2 | 9 | 16 | 23/30 |
| M | | 3 | 10 | 17 | 24/31 |
| Tu | | 4 | 11 | 18 | 25 |
| W | | 5 | 12 | 19 | 26 |
| Th | | 6 | 13 | 20 | 27 |
| F | | 7 | 14 | 21 | 28 |
| Sa | 1 | 8 | 15 | 22 | 29 |

## February

| | | | | | |
|---|---|---|---|---|---|
| Su | | 6 | 13 | 20 | 27 |
| M | | 7 | 14 | 21 | 28 |
| Tu | 1 | 8 | 15 | 22 | |
| W | 2 | 9 | 16 | 23 | |
| Th | 3 | 10 | 17 | 24 | |
| F | 4 | 11 | 18 | 25 | |
| Sa | 5 | 12 | 19 | 26 | |

## May

| | | | | | |
|---|---|---|---|---|---|
| Su | 1 | 8 | 15 | 22 | 29 |
| M | 2 | 9 | 16 | 23 | 30 |
| Tu | 3 | 10 | 17 | 24 | 31 |
| W | 4 | 11 | 18 | 25 | |
| Th | 5 | 12 | 19 | 26 | |
| F | 6 | 13 | 20 | 27 | |
| Sa | 7 | 14 | 21 | 28 | |

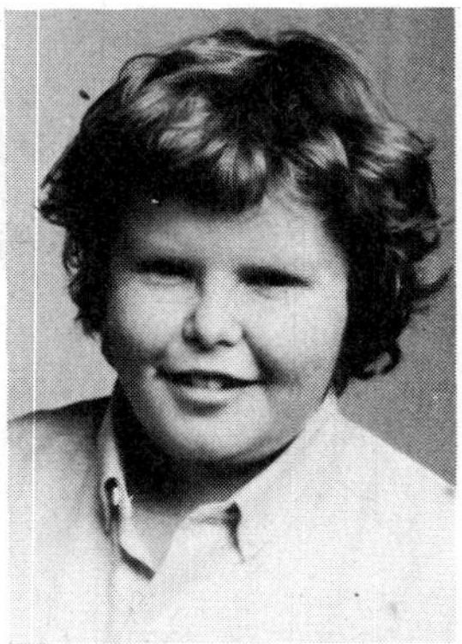

## June

| | | | | | |
|---|---|---|---|---|---|
| Su | | 5 | 12 | 19 | 26 |
| M | | 6 | 13 | 20 | 27 |
| Tu | | 7 | 14 | 21 | 28 |
| W | 1 | 8 | 15 | 22 | 29 |
| Th | 2 | 9 | 16 | 23 | 30 |
| F | 3 | 10 | 17 | 24 | |
| Sa | 4 | 11 | 18 | 25 | |

## September

| | | | | | |
|---|---|---|---|---|---|
| Su | | 4 | 11 | 18 | 25 |
| M | | 5 | 12 | 19 | 26 |
| Tu | | 6 | 13 | 20 | 27 |
| W | | 7 | 14 | 21 | 28 |
| Th | 1 | 8 | 15 | 22 | 29 |
| F | 2 | 9 | 16 | 23 | 30 |
| Sa | 3 | 10 | 17 | 24 | |

## October

| | | | | | |
|---|---|---|---|---|---|
| Su | | 2 | 9 | 16 | 23/30 |
| M | | 3 | 10 | 17 | 24/31 |
| Tu | | 4 | 11 | 18 | 25 |
| W | | 5 | 12 | 19 | 26 |
| Th | | 6 | 13 | 20 | 27 |
| F | | 7 | 14 | 21 | 28 |
| Sa | 1 | 8 | 15 | 22 | 29 |

# CALENDAR 1983

## March

| | | | | | |
|---|---|---|---|---|---|
| Su | | 6 | 13 | 20 | 27 |
| M | | 7 | 14 | 21 | 28 |
| Tu | 1 | 8 | 15 | 22 | 29 |
| W | 2 | 9 | 16 | 23 | 30 |
| Th | 3 | 10 | 17 | 24 | 31 |
| F | 4 | 11 | 18 | 25 | |
| Sa | 5 | 12 | 19 | 26 | |

## April

| | | | | | |
|---|---|---|---|---|---|
| Su | | 3 | 10 | 17 | 24 |
| M | | 4 | 11 | 18 | 25 |
| Tu | | 5 | 12 | 19 | 26 |
| W | | 6 | 13 | 20 | 27 |
| Th | | 7 | 14 | 21 | 28 |
| F | 1 | 8 | 15 | 22 | 29 |
| Sa | 2 | 9 | 16 | 23 | 30 |

## July

| | | | | | |
|---|---|---|---|---|---|
| Su | | 3 | 10 | 17 | 24/31 |
| M | | 4 | 11 | 18 | 25 |
| Tu | | 5 | 12 | 19 | 26 |
| W | | 6 | 13 | 20 | 27 |
| Th | | 7 | 14 | 21 | 28 |
| F | 1 | 8 | 15 | 22 | 29 |
| Sa | 2 | 9 | 16 | 23 | 30 |

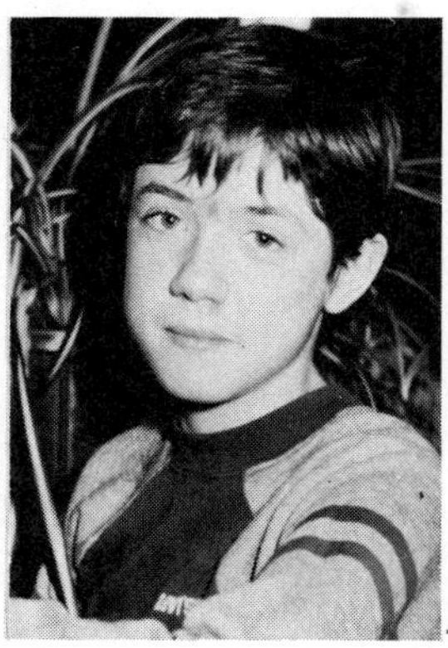

## August

| | | | | | |
|---|---|---|---|---|---|
| Su | | 7 | 14 | 21 | 28 |
| M | 1 | 8 | 15 | 22 | 29 |
| Tu | 2 | 9 | 16 | 23 | 30 |
| W | 3 | 10 | 17 | 24 | 31 |
| Th | 4 | 11 | 18 | 25 | |
| F | 5 | 12 | 19 | 26 | |
| Sa | 6 | 13 | 20 | 27 | |

## November

| | | | | | |
|---|---|---|---|---|---|
| Su | | 6 | 13 | 20 | 27 |
| M | | 7 | 14 | 21 | 28 |
| Tu | 1 | 8 | 15 | 22 | 29 |
| W | 2 | 9 | 16 | 23 | 30 |
| Th | 3 | 10 | 17 | 24 | |
| F | 4 | 11 | 18 | 25 | |
| Sa | 5 | 12 | 19 | 26 | |

## December

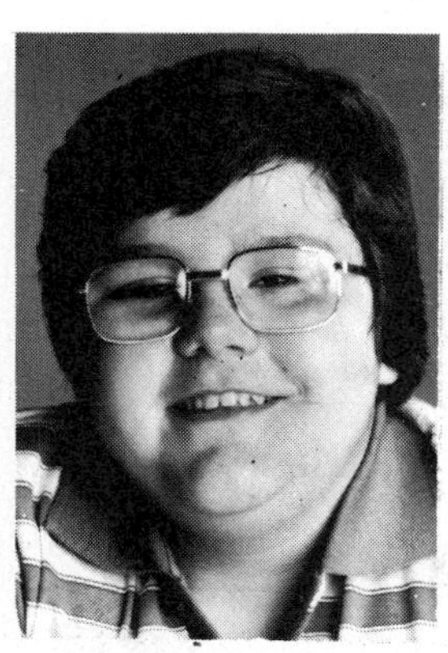

| | | | | | |
|---|---|---|---|---|---|
| Su | | 4 | 11 | 18 | 25 |
| M | | 5 | 12 | 19 | 26 |
| Tu | | 6 | 13 | 20 | 27 |
| W | | 7 | 14 | 21 | 28 |
| Th | 1 | 8 | 15 | 22 | 29 |
| F | 2 | 9 | 16 | 23 | 30 |
| Sa | 3 | 10 | 17 | 24 | 31 |

# A LAUGH AN' A HALF!

**If you know any school jokes, don't forget to send 'em in. The more the better!**

☆

A teacher decided to teach a know-all pupil a lesson. In history, she asked him on which date the Titanic sank. The boy answered correctly. "Now, she said, "how many passengers were on board?" Again he gave the right answer. "And now for my last question," she smiled, "tell me—what were their names?"

●

**Teacher**: "Do you like Shakespeare?"
**Pupil**: "Dunno, Miss—never been to the seaside!"

●

**Teacher**: "What is a wombat for?"
**Pupil**: "Playing wom?"

●

**Teacher**: "What is a yokel?"
**Pupil**: "The centre of an eggle!"

**Teacher**: "You should have been here at nine!"
**Pupil**: "Why, what happened?"

●

**Mum**: "Are you the young teacher who saved my son from drowning when he fell through the ice?"
**Teacher**: "Yes, Ma'am."
**Mum**: "Well, where are his mittens?"

●

**Teacher**: "Now, who is going on the school outing?"
**Boy**: "Well, *I* ain't going!"
**Teacher**: "No, Peter, that is wrong. It should be: 'I am not going, you are not going, he is not going, they are not going . . .' "
**Boy**: "Blimey, ain't nobody going?"

●

Have you heard about the girl who was mad about P.E. and fitness? She sat up all night studying for a blood test!

**Boy**: "Er—hi, Dad. I—er—failed my O-levels, nicked the Head's car, got expelled from my boarding school, burnt down the physics lab, and the police are after me! 'Fraid you ain't gonna be too pleased."
**Dad**: "Pleased? Pleased? Is this the reward I get for slaving and sacrificing for you? Ten years at the poshest, most expensive schools in the country—and you still say 'ain't'!"

●

**Pupil**: "What are you going to do with the school piano?"
**Man**: "Going to tune it, son!"
**Pupil**: "Does that make it go faster?"

●

**Q. What do you call a teacher with a new type of extra-strong cane?**
A. "Sir"!

●

**Voice**: "Mummy, I'm *not* getting up to go to school today."
**Mum**: "Yes you will, dear."
**Voice**: "Won't, won't won't! I—I'll hold my breath, I'll bite my fingers off, I'll . . ."
**Mum**: "Don't be silly, dear!"
**Voice**: "I—I'm scared. The teachers hate me, the kids hate me . . . tell me *why* I should go?"
**Mum**: "Well, you *are* the Head, dear!"

●

**Girl**: "Sir, there's a man at the door with a bill."
**Teacher**: "Be sensible, Gillian, it must be a duck, with a hat on!"

●

**Dad**: "I hear you're the teacher's pet, son, is this true?"
**Boy**: "Don't be daft, he's called Rover!"

## SILLY SCHOOL BOOKS

"The Empty Classroom" by Juliet Garlic.
"Double Mathematics" by Rex A. Day.
"The Missing Books" by Hugh Adam Last.
"School Discipline" by Laura Norder.
"Parted Friends" by Wendy Bellgoes.
"Mercy On Pupils!" by Grant A. Pardon.
"Tough Subject? Keep Trying!" by Percy Vere.
"Beware Of Your Teacher!" by Sheila Tack.
"School Hold-up" by Stan Andy Liver.
"Boring Lessons" by Mona Lott.
"Start To Write" by Nick A. Pen.
"The Lazy Pupil" by Betty Slate.
"Caning" by Ben Down & Phil Paine.
"Runaway Teacher" by Gladys Gone.
"School Dinners" by Nora Bone.
"A Fall In The Gym" by Denise R. Week.
"Seeing The Head" by Oliver Tremble.
"School Dinners—A Waste?" by May I. Leavit.
"Books Are Unnecessary!" by Chuck M. Down.
"Confessions Of A Delinquent" by I. Dunnett.
"Keep Your Work Clean" by Hans Mark Whiting.
"Playing Truant" by C.U. Later.
"The Teacher's Pet" by Miles Toogood.
"Drinking In Class" by Dwain D. Canfast.
"Punctuality" by Earl E. Bird.

## THE SCHOOL DOCTOR'S VISIT

P. "Doctor, Doctor, I think I'm a stick of coloured chalk!"
D. "You look all white to me!"

•

P. "Doctor, Doctor, I think I'm an exercise book!"
D. "If you turn over a new leaf, I'll write you a prescription!"

•

P. "Doctor, Doctor, I'm getting an obsession that a netball's going to land on my head!"
D. "Don't worry—I think I've caught it in time!"

P. "Doctor, Doctor, I keep thinking I'm a trampoline!"
D. "Don't jump the queue!"

•

P. "Doctor, Doctor, I think I'm a school glove!"
D. "Hold on, and I'll give you a hand!"

•

P. "Doctor, Doctor, I keep thinking I'm a tennis ball!"
D. "Serves you right!"

•

P. "Doctor, Doctor, I think I'm a school library book!"
D. "Well, hurry back, before you're overdue!"

•

P. Doctor, Doctor, whenever I put my hat on, I hear music!"
D. "Well, that's no problem! I'll take the band out!"

•

P. "Doctor, Doctor, I keep thinking I'm a school cap!"
D. "Get on ahead, and I'll follow you later!"

•

P. "Doctor, Doctor, the other kids think I'm a blackboard!"
D. "So what's the problem?"
P. "They keep giving me the brush-off!"

# Okay, let's hear 'em...

# YOUR MOANS

***Read some other worried* Grange Hill *fans' problems and you might find answers to a few of your own . . .***

## THE UNIFORM'S HORRIBLE

● **One of the teachers at my school is always getting at me for not wearing our full school uniform. I wouldn't mind if it was okay, but it's a really foul-coloured dark green which makes me look awful. Honestly, I wouldn't be seen dead in it! What's worse, my boyfriend sometimes meets me after school, so I daren't dash out looking grotty.**

*Michelle, Leyton.*

Sorry, Michelle, but if your school rules state that you must wear uniform at school, then you must. All you've got to do to keep your teacher happy is wear your uniform during the day. On the nights that you know your fella's picking you up, do a quick change in the loo. Couldn't be easier!

And one more thing, everyone thinks they look dreadful in school uniform, but it's not always true! You may even find that your boyfriend thinks it looks okay.

## NO CHOICE OF SCHOOL

● **I want to go to a local school where all my mates are going next term, only my parents insist I must take a bus and train ride to the comprehensive right on the other side of town. Seems pretty stupid to me!**

**I've tried talking to them, but they won't listen. I'm so fed up, I'm thinking of writing to our Local Education Authority to see if they can get Mum and Dad to change their minds.**

*Vince, Birmingham.*

Well, it would be a waste of time if you did. Sorry, Vince. Up until you're eighteen years old, your parents can actually make you go to the school of their choice. And they obviously think the school that's further away is for the best, otherwise they wouldn't insist on you making such a long journey twice a day for no reason.

Try to make the most of a bad deal. You can still see your mates at weekends—and in the evenings. And you'll be bound to make lots of new ones at your new school. Keep an optimistic view if you can.

## SHOULD I LIE?

● **Our school's got an awful reputation locally for having rough pupils. I'm not one of them, but I'm scared that when I leave next year, I might be looked on as a trouble-maker by future employers. Jobs are hard enough to get as it is without admitting which school I have been attending. So do you think it would be a good idea to lie to them and make out I'd been to another, nicer school? It'd only be a white lie.**

*Barbie, Swansea.*

No! Because they would eventually find out you'd lied to them—and that would go against you far more than the reputation of your school—however tarnished it is.

In any case, your fears are probably exaggerated. The school might have a bad reputation, but most people will realise that that reputation doesn't apply to all its pupils. So work hard and get as many qualifications as you can—because they're the things that really count.

## HE'S PICKING ON ME

● **I'm being picked on by the maths teacher at my school. He's always getting me to run errands for him. Last week, I even had to carry his bag for him up the stairs. He doesn't ask any of the others to do it. Do you think he picks on me because I'm useless in his lessons? And do I have to do what he says?**

*Steve, Watford.*

'Fraid you do have to obey him, Steve. In school, your teachers have the same rights as your parents, so this guy can tell you what to do and make sure that you do it. Also, his attitude could be because he thinks you're not *trying* in his lessons. Think it over . . .

There's a lot of difference between being bad at maths and making no effort. Why not try a bit harder? If you don't understand something—tell him so. Don't just sit there and say nothing, that won't get you anywhere.

Your relationship should improve, but if you still find yourself running round after him and think his behaviour is unreasonable, get your parents to speak to the Head. They can explain the situation.

## AM I A BABY?

● **All the girls in my class smoke in the lunch hour. I hate cigarettes, so I've never even wanted to join in. I don't mind being the odd one out, but they really make me feel bad about it by calling me a baby and a coward. It's getting to the point where I almost feel like taking a drag just to keep them quiet.**

*Julia, Bromley.*

Well, that would be plain stupid. It's

# AND GROANS

going to be hard, but you've got to put up with the teasing and stick by your beliefs. Although you're having a hard time right now, you'll be grateful that you didn't lose your resolve in the long run.

You don't have to be told how bad smoking is for your health. Maybe you should tell your friends, though. It would be a favour.

You could also remind them of the laws about smoking. They are that you're not allowed to buy cigarettes or smoke them in public if you're under sixteen.

## NOWHERE TO GO

● **At my school they seem to dole out homeword by the ton. I wouldn't mind, it's just that I've got nowhere to concentrated at home. I share my room with my two brothers.**

*Roger, Newcastle.*

You could try sitting in the kitchen where it's quiet. If not, ask your teachers for permission to stay an hour or so after school.

## WHAT A BORE!

● **I'm desperate to leave school. It's so boring and I've learnt all there is to know. Trouble is, I've been told that I won't even be able to leave school at sixteen because my birthday's at the wrong time of the year.**

*Jon, Cheshire.*

Whoever told you this information had his or her facts wrong. You can leave at sixteen, but the actual date does depend, as you were told, on what time of year your birthday falls.

The rule is, if your birthday is between September 1 and January 31, you leave at Easter after your sixteenth birthday. But if your birthday is at any other time, you have to wait to the end of May.

Incidentally, though, Jon—you're probably finding school so dreary because of your attitude. It's impossible to know *all* there is to know. People go on learning for their whole lifetime.

Think about it . . . and try to find some subject that does interest you.

## IT'S REVOLTING MUCK

● **The meals dished up at my school aren't fit for pigs. The meat's revolting, the vegetables are always overcooked and the puddings are disgusting. I want to take sandwiches, but my mum won't let me because she works and can't be bothered to cook me a meal when she gets home. Any suggestions?**

*Avril, Somerset.*

Yes—several. The first is to stop moaning and do something about the situation yourself.

It's probably not that your mum can't be bothered to cook you a meal—no doubt she's just too exhausted after a long day at work.

Naturally, she's worried that you should get a proper meal each day, and that's why she insists on you taking school dinners.

If they're really that unbearable, why not suggest that you make your own sandwiches in the morning and offer to lend a hand with the evening meal? We don't only mean preparing the vegetables either, you must also be willing to help out with the extra shopping it'll involve . . .

## MY MUM'S HAD ENOUGH

● **There are these big lads at school who go round cutting off us younger boys' ties. Well, it's happened to me so many times now that I've lost count. The trouble is, my mum's getting really fed-up with buying me new ones. She said it's got to stop and that if I don't go to the Head, she will. I'm scared the bullies will find out.**

*David, Leeds.*

She's right, you know, David. Bullies shouldn't be allowed to get away with their behaviour. Especially, if it's at the expense of others. Why should your poor mum carry on forking out?

It *is* time you were brave enough to have a chat with one of your teachers about what's been going on. Choose one who you know will be discreet enough not to 'split' on you. That way the boys responsible need never know who reported them.

## THEY CALL US NAMES

● **My problem is one of my teachers. You see, he just happens to be my dad. He never picks me out for special treatment or anything, but some of the other kids reckon he does. They call us both names and I get very upset. What can I do?**

*Valli, Berkshire.*

This really is an awkward situation. Some people will always believe a parent teacher is likely to treat their son or daughter better than the other pupils. And it's really a problem that's too big for you to cope with alone.

Please have a word with your father and let him know what's going on. All teachers are called names, but it's unfair that you should suffer as well.

A lot of schools don't even allow parents to teach their own children—so your Head must be aware of the situation—and hopefully he'll be able to put things right. The solution maybe to transfer you to a different class for the lessons your dad takes.

*Unfortunately, it is impossible to answer problem letters personally. If you need advice on something that's troubling you, go to an older person who you can trust. That could be a parent, aunt or uncle, teacher or even a sister or brother.*

# HORRIBLE HOMEWORK!

***No, you'll enjoy the brain strain really when you try these puzzles.***

## 1. QUICK CROSSWORD

**CLUES ACROSS**
**1 Large Australian animal which protects its young in a pouch**
**5 Alone, as in singing alone**
**7 Sodium chloride, or the accompaniment to pepper!**
**8 Canvas structure for camping**
**9 The opposite of more**
**11 Several of these make a flight of stairs**
**12 To desire or long for something**
**13 A mixture of cement, sand and water used for building**

**CLUES DOWN**
**2 The container built by a bird for its eggs**
**3 Every plant has at least one of these under the ground**
**4 The greatest river in India**
**6 A deer's horn**
**10 Large graceful water bird**
**11 A covering for the foot**

Turn to page 79 for the answers to all these tricky questions. Only if you've solved them all, though!

## 2. SCRAMBLED SUBJECTS

*The nine jumbled-up words below are anagrams of school subjects. Un-scramble each anagram and write it into the grid. When complete, another anagram will appear in the shaded squares reading downwards. What should it read?*

**1 Chsipyh**
**2 Tra**
**3 Sniehlg**
**4 Ooiblyg**
**5 Nhfcer**
**6 Yhoagergp**
**7 Esagm**
**8 Sohrtiy**
**9 Etsmihacmat**

Just one clue! The first one's Physics.

## 3. GOOD SPORTS

Listed from 1 to 10 below are some well-known sportsmen and women. Listed alongside from A to J are the sports for which each of them is well-known. But the two lists have been shuffled, so match up the numbered person with the correct letter of their sport.

| | | | |
|---|---|---|---|
| 1 | **Sharron Davies** | A | **Cricket** |
| 2 | **Justin Fashanu** | B | **Tennis** |
| 3 | **Nelli Kim** | C | **Motorbike racing** |
| 4 | **John Watson** | D | **Swimming** |
| 5 | **Tracy Austin** | E | **Football** |
| 6 | **Ian Botham** | F | **Golf** |
| 7 | **Linsey Macdonald** | G | **Gymnastics** |
| 8 | **Randy Mamola** | H | **Horse riding** |
| 9 | **Lucinda Prior-Palmer** | I | **Athletics** |
| 10 | **Severiano Ballesteros** | J | **Motor racing** |

# 4. LUCKY NUMBERS

$\boxed{11} \times \boxed{5} + \boxed{3} \div \boxed{2} + \boxed{9} - \boxed{12} \times \boxed{4} - \boxed{9} \div \boxed{5} - \boxed{4} = \boxed{11}$

The answer to each of the ten questions below is a number. Fill in the numbers in the boxes as you answer them and complete the arithmetic, adding, dividing, multiplying and so on until you come to the final figure.

**1. How many players in a hockey team?**
**2. How many senses do you have?**
**3. How many Police members?**
**4. A bird in the hand is worth how many in the bush?**
**5. How many known planets in the solar system?**
**6. How many days of Christmas?**
**7. How many suits in a pack of cards?**
**8. A stitch in time saves how many?**
**9. How many legs has a starfish?**
**10. How many wonders of the world are there meant to be?**

# 5. CITY LIMITS

***Listed here are eleven capital cities. Identify the country of which they are the capital and strike out the initial letter of that country's name from the box of letters. You'll be left with some odd letters that spell out a language.***

| | | | |
|---|---|---|---|
| D | K | C | T |
| A | G | S | J |
| I | A | L | I |
| A | N | C | A |

**MADRID**
**TOKYO**
**NEW DELHI**
**COPENHAGEN**
**VIENNA**
**OTTAWA**
**CANBERRA**
**NAIROBI**
**BUENOS AIRES**
**PEKING**
**ATHENS**

# 6. STAR PUPILS

***Can you fill in the missing letters to make up a few** Grange hill **pupils' real names? You should be good!***

**1 -O-- C--T-**
**2 S--A-N- -O-S**
**3 L-- -P-R--**
**4 -E- ---D-N--D**
**5 T-R-- -U- P--T**
**6 E-K-- -U-T-F-**

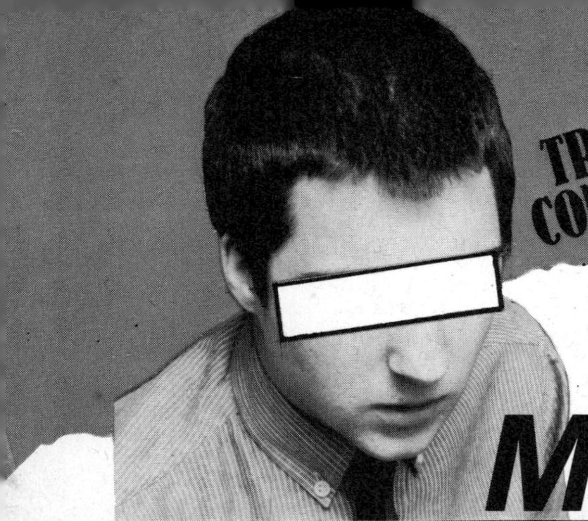

TRUE-LIFE CONFESSION

***Peter Jackson had a private war going on with his teacher—and both were determined they'd be the one to win . . .***

# 'I PUNCHED MY TEACHER!'

**It's hard to believe I'm sitting here in a police station. It seems like a bad dream that I'm going to wake up from in a minute. But then I look around at the bare walls, the man in uniform behind the desk, and I know it's all for real.**

It started as soon as I went into Saunders' class. I'd never been any good at English, and I couldn't help getting bored at him reading poetry most of the time.

The other thing that got me was that he always acted like he wanted to be mates with you. He'd keep cracking silly jokes, and we'd laugh at them to humour him. And then he'd suddenly decide he wanted to 'get down to some hard work', and when we kept larking about, he started handing out punishments instead.

## ACTED

Anyway, he never fooled me. All this 'being mates' didn't mean anything. He had this big flash car, a nice house outside town and a stuck-up wife. Very flippin' cosy. Outside of school he wouldn't have wanted to know me!

There are six kids in my family. My two elder brothers are both on the dole. Dad went off years ago, and Mum's always out playing bingo or drinking with her men friends.

I didn't like the way old Saunders always seemed to be talking down to me. So what if he'd read up about some bloke called Shakespeare? Didn't make him better than me, did it?

So I kept mucking about in Saunders' lessons. I used to sit at the back with the other blokes at school. The kids who sat at the back were always the tough ones.

I'd never really been accepted as a proper part of the crowd, though. The real nutjobs were a closed sort of circle. I don't know where they got their money, but they always seemed to have plenty to splash about.

And they could chat up the girls, too. I always seemed to be useless when it came to pulling talent. These blokes didn't tell me to push off or anything, but I could see they didn't really want me hanging around them.

Then, after a couple of weeks in Saunders' class, he started making these sarcastic remarks to me.

I'd just made one of my little jokes, and I was feeling pretty good 'cos all the tough guys were laughing, and then old Saunders said, "Well, Jackson, I can see you're a real wit. I think you could become a best selling novelist one day. The only problem is that you don't know how to read or write." Well, there were a few giggles at this, so I said, "Oh, what a shame, Sir. I s'pose I'll just have to settle for being an English teacher!"

Everybody roared at that one, but Saunders went red in the face. He came up to me and started prodding me in the chest. He gave me a real mouthful. But I just sat there and grinned. I wasn't going to let him get the better of me, and after the lesson, the tough blokes came up to me and told me that I'd given old Saunders what for.

After that though, Saunders really had it in for me. He was taunting me all the time. And I kept trying to crack my little jokes back. He seemed to be trying to put me down over and over again. But I couldn't let him do that. If he got the better of me, everyone would laugh and I'd look a right blinkin' wally.

## CRYING

But he did have the upper hand. It got so I dreaded going into his class. Then one day I decided to bunk off. I had a double lesson with Saunders, and I couldn't face it. Trouble was, at dinner time I went out for some chips, and who should pass me in his car but Saunders. Next day I was in the Head's office getting caned for it.

But the worst thing was when I went back to the class, Saunders started gloating.

"Well, if it isn't the witty Jackson," he said. He walked over to my desk. "Red around the eyes, eh? Been crying, I shouldn't wonder. Not such a tough guy after all, eh, Jackson?"

I didn't answer.

"I said not such a tough guy after all, eh?" he said, prodding me in the chest.

## SIREN

Everybody was laughing. I could hear them all. It felt like my head would burst with the noise of it. And through it all I could feel Saunders' finger poking me in the chest, and I could hear his voice, taunting me over and over again. I had my hands in my pockets and I clenched my fists. 'Once more,' I thought. 'You just poke me once more.' And then before I knew it, I'd lifted up my right arm and punched him straight in the face.

Suddenly all the noise seemed to stop. I was on my feet and looking down at Saunders who had fallen backwards, hitting his head on a radiator.

There was a trickle of blood running down his forehead, and his eyes were closed. For a moment, I thought he was dead.

Eventually other teachers came rushing into the classroom. There was the siren of a police car and the scream of an ambulance. I remember thinking that it was funny that I'd caused so much fuss.

So here I am sitting in this Police station. They told me I was lucky that Saunders only had bad concussion and a suspected broken jaw.

But I wish it had never happened. They'll charge me with grievous bodily harm or something, I know it. There's no way I'm not guilty. And with a record, what chance will I have of getting a decent job now? I'll just have to sit here and sweat it out, I suppose, but all I do is keep asking myself the same thing: "You idiot, why did you do it? Why did you do such a stupid thing . . .?"

## GORDON JONAH JONES
**(Lee Sparke)**

BIRTHDAY: 20th February, 1969 STAR SIGN: Pisces
FAVOURITE FOOD: Steak, chips and all the trimmings!
HOBBIES: Swimming—Lee used to collect coins, too, but finds it boring now PETS: 2 cats, Tinkerbell and Sooty BROTHERS: 1 older, Dane SISTERS: None OTHER APPEARANCES: In the TV series, *Thomas and Sarah,* and lots of commercials including one for hamburgers and another for chocolate biscuits

# Big spender

***It came as a bit of a shock to Zammo when he suddenly found himself loaded with money. Twenty five pounds seemed like a real fortune to spend. . .***

**The Zargon invasion of Earth wasn't quite the same without the sound. Zammo's mum had turned it down to hear herself nagging.**

**"Sixteen days 'til Christmas," she sighed, running her iron over one of Dad's shirts. The telly ads had reminded her. "And I bet you haven't started thinking about presents!"**

**She was wrong there. Zammo'd thought about what he'd like and he'd dropped a few hints. What she was getting at, though, was what he was going to give. That had crossed his mind, too, for a few seconds. The trouble was, presents cost money and Zammo was constantly broke so it hardly seemed worth making out a list.**

"Jessica and Margaret buy presents from their pocket money. Why can't you?"

She always got on at him when his dad was working late. Zammo kept quiet. Alien megacruisers were raining down on New York, silently reducing skyscrapers to groundscrapers with blinding flashes of laser power. The guys at Space Control were running around like demented ants.

"You're not listening to me!" said a bulky figure in a frayed pink housecoat, barging between him and the box. The button clicked off, obliterating Commander Crabbe's last message to the universe. "It's high time you started thinking of others, instead of just yourself," his mum said, leaning towards him.

"Aaaw, you'll get your presents, don't you worry!" Zammo scowled, getting to his feet and slouching out of the room. He headed upstairs to his usual retreat whenever there was any aggravation.

So what if his sisters had started saving? All you ever got from them was a bar of chocolate in a pretty wrapper. They expected a bit more from him, seeing as he got twice their pocket money.

He switched on his trannie and lay back on his bed. It wasn't as if he was greedy. His money just didn't seem to last very long. Now, if he had a spare twenty quid or so right now, things would be different!

## PRIZE

As if to put his good intentions to the test, Fate provided him with that just two days later.

"Hey, a cheque for twenty-five pounds!" his mum gasped one morning before he'd left for school. She'd torn open a light brown envelope addressed to her. "On the Premium Bonds!"

It took Zammo five seconds to work out that the money was his. No-one in their house held any Premium Bonds except him. He remembered moaning when he'd been given them by daft old Aunt Nelly. The silly old bat had bought them in his mum's name 'cos she thought he wasn't old enough to hold them. Trust her to get it all wrong. At the time, he'd rather have had the money anyway. Didn't reckon he stood much chance of winning a prize. But now . . .

"Seems like this is our lucky year then, doesn't it, Sammy," his mother smiled.

"Guess so," he replied, wondering how it involved her.

"For once, you will be able to buy us presents!"

Zammo nearly choked on his toast. He'd already earmarked that money for a portable Space Invaders game.

"Dunno if I'll be able to cash it in time," he mumbled, hoping that these things took weeks.

His mum wasn't daft enough to fall for that line.

"*You* don't have to cash it. *I* do, because it has my name on it!" She picked the cheque off the table. "In fact, since we've actually got the money right here in our hands, your father and I are prepared to lend you the twenty-five pounds in advance. Isn't that right, George!"

*"Blimey, what you got there?" Jonah gasped, looking at the parcels.*

Zammo's father muttered something as he put on his coat. It was the first time he'd heard of it, but he hadn't time to argue. He was late for work.

"You can do your Christmas shopping tomorrow morning," his mum pointed out, the next day being Saturday.

That settled it.

* * * * *

Shopping in the High Street was always murder on a Saturday. Knowing that he was getting little out of it for himself made it worse for Zammo. He'd spent half the night awake working out what to buy each of the family. He wanted to strike the right balance between being mean and going overboard. After all, the main aim of the exercise was to salvage as much of the money as he could for himself, while at the same time doing enough to shut the mouths of his moaning relatives for the next twelve months.

Some kind of perfume for his mum, he reckoned. She'd like that. His dad had hinted at pyjamas, so he'd better get him some. As for his two sisters, Jessica would probably like a doll and Margaret some kind of game. He'd estimated what they would all cost and decided he'd be left with a tenner.

Two hours' footslogging later, he'd bought the four presents but they'd all cost more than he'd expected. Zammo was lucky to escape with a fiver!

It was as he was shoving his way out of the last toy shop that he met Jonah and his mum. They were waiting at the exit for Jonah's brother Kevin who was having a gander inside.

"Blimey, what you got there?" Jonah gasped, looking at the parcels in Zammo's hands.

## ENVIOUS

Zammo told him, bragging a bit about his own generosity. He could see Mrs. Jones giving her son envious looks.

"Gerroff!" Jonah sneered. "When did you ever give your lot pressies? I remember last year . . .

"That was last year," Zammo cut in. "This year's different. Won some money, didn't I!"

Jonah didn't believe him. Bet he was doing his mum's Christmas shopping and didn't want to admit it. In the end, Zammo angrily vowed to bring his cheque to school on Monday to prove it. Then he strode off fuming.

Back home, he sneaked his parcels upstairs to his room and hid them.

* * * * *

"See?" he said to Jonah first thing on Monday morning. "What did I tell you?" He flashed the cheque which he'd borrowed from behind the clock on the mantelpiece. He hoped his mum wouldn't look for it.

"You said *you* won the money! That's got your mum's name on it!" Jonah jeered.

Zammo tried to explain about batty Aunt Nelly without success. Anyway, what did he care whether Jonah believed him or not. *He* knew he had won. Their raised voices began to attract people's attention.

"What's the argument?" asked Joey Hinds, N1's super-snoop. He was always poking his nose in where it wasn't wanted. "Got something hidden in your pocket, McGuire?"

"Get lost, Hinds! What's it got to do with you?" Zammo snarled as he marched off across the playground.

The trouble with Hinds was that once something had aroused his curiosity, he just had to find out about it. And since neither Jonah nor Zammo would split, he took the first opportunity to do some nosing around.

That presented itself at the end of the P.E. lesson when, after volunteering, Hinds found himself sent back to the changing room to unlock the door ahead of the others. Searching through Zammo's pockets, Hinds soon found the cheque. What a let-down! He'd expected something a bit more interesting.

Suddenly, he heard voices coming into the room. The others had caught him up quicker than he'd expected. He hadn't time to stuff the cheque back where he'd found it, so he rammed it down the front of his shorts and ambled over to his own peg.

The first thing Zammo did when he came back into the room was check his pockets. His stomach hit the floor when he discovered his cheque had gone.

Hinds watched quietly and realised that the balloon would soon go up. As Zammo re-checked his pockets for the second time, Joey Hinds sidled towards the toilet. One quick shredding operation and a flushed toilet pan later, he reappeared, looking decidedly relieved. Zammo had started to raise the alarm and get everyone looking for the cheque.

"Trust you, McGuire, to leave something valuable lying around!" sighed Bullet Baxter. "Okay, no-one leaves this room until it's found!" A thorough person to person search didn't turn it up though, so Zammo had to make his own guesses as to where it had gone.

"Blimey, my mum'll go spare!" he groaned on his way home. His only consoling thought was that, as the Head had pointed out, a new cheque could be obtained. She doubted if the stolen one would be of use to the thief. She hoped it would be a lesson . . .

"I wonder how long it takes to get another cheque? Maybe if I

*He'd borrowed the cheque from behind the clock on the mantelpiece.*

phoned them . . ." Zammo fretted, trying to find a way out before he got home.

"It's bound to take a week or so," Jonah decided, not one to live on false hopes.

"If I ever find out who took it, I'll beat his head in!"

"That's if your dad doesn't beat yours in first!"

"Very funny!" Zammo walked up his garden path like someone on their way to a school exam.

His mum grabbed him as soon as he entered the door.

"Where is it?" she demanded.

"I left it behind the clock!"

For a few seconds, sheer terror almost made him run for it, but he knew it wouldn't do any good. She could tell by the look on his face that he knew all about it.

"Stolen?" his father cried when he got home. "What about our twenty-five quid?"

"You'll get it back. The Bonds Office will issue a new cheque. The Head said so."

"Well, you'd better get writing to them, my lad, because you're not getting any more pocket money 'til we've been paid!"

## NAGGING

If anything prompted Zammo to write straight away and mail his letter first class, that did. Life wasn't worth living without pocket money, even though he still had his fiver left over from his spending spree. It wouldn't last long once the holidays began.

A week later, there was still no reply. The faces at the breakfast table got longer and longer until, finally, one morning, the newspaper boy delivered the news that the postman could not.

"They're on a go slow up there!" Zammo's dad announced as he glanced at the paper.

"Up where?"

"Up there at the Bonds Office. Look, it says so here. No wonder we haven't heard from them," he frowned, handing the paper to his wife.

"That means our money mightn't come for weeks!" she wailed. "And we could have done with the cash over Christmas!"

Zammo felt rotten about it all but there was nothing he could do. He'd said sorry lots of times but it hadn't stopped his mum nagging for a week or so. Still, as Christmas approached, she laid off him a bit. Resigned to waiting,

*"Merry Christmas, Sammy!" said a voice.*

he assumed.

At least he'd got them all decent pressies. They couldn't complain about that this year. He'd even taken the trouble to wrap them up nicely, with bows and labels and pretty paper with reindeer galloping all over it.

On Christmas Eve, he proudly carried his batch down to the sitting room table and placed the gifts next to the artificial tree with the fairy lights. He could feel the inquisitive eyes watching him, wanting to know what was inside. Well, they'd know in the morning. It was a rule in their house that they didn't get their presents 'til Christmas day.

As he left the room, something troubled him slightly. Where were the others' presents? Normally, they were out by now.

* * * * *

The alarm hadn't even gone off the following morning when the whole house was awakened by shouts and the sound of ripping paper downstairs. The two girls were at the parcels.

"Thanks ever so much, Sammy," beamed his youngest sister, giving him a hug as he strolled into the sitting room, only half awake.

"Ta lots, Sammy," echoed Margaret, the contents of her robot game all over the floor.

He sauntered over to the table and was rather shocked by the incredibly small parcels addressed to himself. He'd heard it said that small was beautiful, but big was better in his opinion.

Cautiously, he peeled back the wrapping on one slim package. Out popped the end of a cheap ballpoint pen . . . twenty pence worth at the most! Then another—a couple of hankies. And a third—a measly Mars bar. The fourth parcel, from his mum, contained a drab pair of socks. He was choked.

"Merry Christmas, Sammy!" said a voice at his shoulder.

He turned sullenly to find the whole family watching him. They were trying hard not to laugh.

"Same to you," he growled.

"Like your presents?" his dad asked innocently.

"What do *you* think?" he replied.

"Sorry, but they're all we could afford, being a bit short . . ."

"No need to rub it in!" he muttered. Surely, they could have done their Christmas shopping before the cheque incident!

"Okay, I think he's had enough," his mum smiled.

He gave her a puzzled look, then suddenly realised they all had their hands behind their backs.

"Taraaaa!" blared his little sisters as they whisked some different parcels from behind their backs. They were rather bigger than the others.

"You rotten lot!" he yelled, latching on to their little game. "You've been having me on!"

"Just thought we'd pull your leg a bit," his dad explained, handing over his proper gift.

"You wait!" Zammo warned. "You wait 'til next year! I'll get you back!"

"Oooh, you mean we're getting presents from you *next year* as well?" his mum gasped. "Proper big spender, he's turning out to be!"

**THE END**

**Todd Carty is as busy *now* as he ever was playing Tucker Jenkins in *Grange Hill*. But does he ever regret leaving the series? Not for a second!**

# Goodbye,

**The day that the school gates at *Grange Hill* shut forever on Tucker Jenkins was a sad day for him and his fans. But, actually, not so sad for Todd Carty, the clever actor who played him.**

As he explained, a little while after leaving, "I just got too old to play the part of a schoolboy. Most of the new characters were only just twelve!!! Some of us were really feeling a bit over the hill—especially the fellas, because all our voices had broken and became very deep.

'It was sad breaking away from all my friends—but in a professional way an actor can't get too upset because it's something you've got to accept. A good part can't go on forever—and hopefully, there are many other roles on offer.

"But, personally, I shall miss *Grange Hill.* It was a bit like belonging to a family. I worked with the same people for five years—and you can't just turn your back on that.

"It's the fans who I feel sorry for. A lot of them were very upset over the cast changes. I know they sent lots of letters of complaint to the BBC. You see, they indentified with us—the girls with Trish and the boys with me. I suppose we were comfortable to them. And viewers don't like change—they like everyone and everything to remain the same. Still, after a while I guess they got used to the new characters and forgot all about us."

There were good and bad points about "being" Tucker, of course. And Todd's life was affected in quite a big way.

# Tucker Jenkins—hello, Todd Carty...

"I really enjoyed the fun times," laughs Todd, "like when I was asked to open a fête. By the end of the day my arm would ache from signing autographs."

Another favourite memory of Todd's was when his little sister gave a birthday party.

"She invited lots of her little friends along from primary school and one of them—her boyfriend—couldn't believe I was actually there. He was really amazed! It was 'Tucker this . . .' and 'Tucker that . . .' all afternoon. And, 'Cor—isn't he tall—wait till I tell my dad.' I, or rather Tucker, really made his day. All the guests asked for my autograph and in the end went off clutching signed pictures of yours truly!"

If younger fans find it difficult to distinguish between a TV role and the real life actor, the problem's not serious. It's altogether different when teenage boys get rather confused in the same way.

**TOUGH**

"Yes," admits Todd. "Threats are still a problem even now. Fellas can be so aggressive when they see me in the street. Because Tucker is quite a tough character, they can't believe I'm not the same person and they want to take a dig at me. It's only a small minority and I get along by ignoring them. But I'll be glad when that's all completely behind me."

Even if *Grange Hill* is over for Todd, life is far from quiet.

"I've been very busy," he told us. "Absolutely no resting periods. One of the first things I did was finish a radio play for the BBC. And before that I did a chat show for LBC. I've also done some radio adverts for a pop magazine, but one thing you won't see or hear is a programme I recorded for German TV called *Force on Britain*.

"There are lots of other exciting things in the pipeline, too—including films. I'd love to tell you all about them—but they're all at the contract stage and I don't want to count my chickens before they're hatched."

Todd's home life has altered, too. He's moved out of his parents' place and is now living in his own flat.

"I love the privacy," he explained. I'm a bit of a loner really. I know people won't believe this but it's true. And I've only got one good friend. Okay, you can have a thousand good companions, but the one good friend is the most important."

Another thing that comes as a surprise is that he hates crowds.

"I'm no party-goer or drinker," he told us. "I just can't stand having a lot of people around me. I'm the quiet sort. I've got my video recorder, my TV, my music and my snooker table all at home and they keep me happy.

"I like theatres very much—and long drives in the country, with or without a girlfriend, depending on how I feel."

To fit in with his loner image, Todd adores taking holidays in Ireland where he's got relatives scattered all over the place. He loves the people and the land.

**AMBITION**

"It's one of the most beautiful places in the world, the countryside is great. So lovely and quiet. It's a good place to visit, I can recommend it. There's a real 'get away from it all' feeling. And the food's terrific, too. The Irish are smashing cooks and they won't let you out of their door until you're stuffed full.

"I enjoy horse-riding now and again—at home and in Ireland. Don't get me wrong—I'm no Lone Ranger, but I manage to stay in the saddle most of the time."

As for future ambition, that's an easy question for Todd to answer.

"My ambition is the same as any other actor's. To be ambitious if you see what I mean."

At this point, Todd had to take his leave. He had an urgent appointment to keep fit.

"Yeah," he grinned. "One of my rooms at home is set up as a gym—you know, the full works, with lots of equipment. I do press-ups, weight lifting, the lot. And while I'm working out, I watch Clint Eastwood films. Well, you never know, I may end up as muscular as him one day!" And with another laugh he was gone.

**Do you have difficulty getting out of bed? Does the thought of another day at school send you diving back under the covers to hide with your teddy? Well, our tips will solve the problem!**

# UP, UP AND AWAY!

1. Bribe your kid brother to chuck cold water over you. Or, save your money and just ask him—it's bound to be a treat!
2. Imagine it's Saturday and *Tiswas* has just started!
3. Sleep with a cold hot water bottle.
4. Buy a large dog and train it to jump on your bed at dawn . . .
5. . . . Or failing that, a large budgie will do!
6. Get your sis to come in and sing Bucks Fizz's greatest hits until you get up.
7. Put an alarm clock in a biscuit tin—on the other side of the room. If the noise of *that* doesn't make you get up, nothing will!
8. Tie your covers to the back bumper of your dad's car. Then, when he drives off to work, he'll take your covers with him—and you'll freeze!
9. Go to bed at eight in the evening. That way, by six in the morning, you'll be dying to get up!
10. Count sheep backwards.
11. Get someone to bring you a nice cuppa . . .
12. Remember that it's bad for you to have *too* much sleep—just as it's important to get enough.
13. Fix up your radio alarm to go off at seven—and remove the "Off" button!
14. Sleep in the kitchen. It may not help you get up, but at least you won't have too far to walk to get your breakfast in the morning!
15. Think of something nice that's happening that day . . .
16. . . . And if that doesn't work, think of the earful the Head's going to give you if you're late!
17. Sleep with a brick under your pillow, it'll be a pleasure to lift your head and get some relief!
18. Sleep standing up.
19. Drink loads of water before you go to bed—you'll be getting up all night!
20. Get up extra early so you can do something you like.
21. Think of that huge breakfast waiting for you!
22. Tape your mum yelling at you to get up. Play it at an even louder decibel than she usually achieves.
23. Put all your clothes out ready so you don't waste time wandering around looking for 'em. Or even better, leave them on when you go to bed! You'll be glad to get up after sleeping in your blazer all night!
24. Grow yourself a very large Venus Fly-Trap plant—and train it to get hungry around seven! Feed it before it eats *you*.
25. Make sure your room's nice and warm before you get up—that way it won't be so bad!

# BOY meets GIRL...

**_Grange Hill_ is a very good example of your average mixed sex school – with its ups and downs and good and bad points.**

And whatever type of school you go to—either mixed or single sex—you probably complain like crazy about the place and reckon it would be much better if it lost or gained a few boys or girls.

Only a few years ago though, life was pretty similar in all schools. Boys and girls were segregated up to the point where they might have been creatures from outer space. Different entrances were used at all times; separate parts of the dining room were sectioned off for meals and breaks were most definitely single sex affairs with separate playgrounds and staff keeping an eagle eye out to make sure the rules were always obeyed.

## HAPPIER

Even today, some schools like that still exist, but thankfully, they are few and far between. Most Heads think mixing with the opposite sex makes for much happier and better balanced kids. And a lot of single sex schools get together with different schools in the area for social and sports gatherings.

But what—if any—are the real advantages and disadvantages of single or mixed schools?

Lucy, 11, recently started at an all-girls' school in South London and thinks it's great . . . apart from certain things!

"Well, to start off with, I've got two brothers so I'm glad to get away from boys. But some of my friends—especially the ones with just sisters—are scared stiff of fellas, so I think it would be a definite advantage for them to meet a few boys. Honestly, I've taken a few of them home and they go all weird if my brothers even look at them. It's really embarrassing because they either start giggling and chattering non-stop, or clam up altogether. My brothers reckon most of my mates are nutters anyway, and I don't blame them with the sample they've seen so far.

"On the plus side, I reckon all-girls' schools give you more confidence. For instance, we put on a school play every year and we do everything ourselves—even down to the lighting and moving props around. Now, if there were boys around, they'd automatically take over the 'men's' jobs and we'd never learn how to fix fuses.

*Which do you believe is better—a mixed school or one where boys or girls go through years of lessons alone? There are arguments for and against both types of schooling! We examine them all here.*

"Another good thing is that when you're with the girls, you don't care so much about how you look. You can dash about on the netball or hockey field and not worry if your hair's gone all frizzy or your mascara's got smudged.

"I suppose the one thing that really does annoy me is that while we have loads of lessons on things like cookery and needlecraft, we don't have any on woodwork or mechanics."

And that's a point that Paul, 12, who goes to a mixed comprehensive in Kent would agree with.

"When I first heard I had the choice of homecraft or woodwork, I fell about laughing. So did all my mates. We all thought the girls would opt for the kitchen bit and the boys for the workroom. But it didn't turn out like that. Loads of boys chose cookery. They came in for a fair bit of stick but I really admired them. I'd have quite liked to have had a go at it myself. Some of them can make chicken pie and chips now!

"Most of us boys thought we'd get a few laughs out of the girls in our woodwork class, too—but one girl has only gone and beaten all of us hands down! It's quite embarrassing watching her knock out a lampstand while we're all still fumbling around with nails and screws.

"Other than that, I don't really think much about the problem. Girls are just there. They're certainly no big deal. I've never seen any of the steamy stockroom sessions that are supposed to go on."

## RELAXED

So, for the record, there is no perfect kind of school. But the main advantage of a mixed school is that, as you get older, you accept boys or girls as people and not just 'dates'. And if you do go out with someone you meet at school, you're not going to be as generally self-conscious as you would be if you'd only just met. Romance doesn't disappear just 'cos you've sat next to someone since the age of ten and shared your homework answers—it can be even better 'cos everything's more relaxed.

What do you think? Write and let us know. We'd like your views.

*Tucker and Cathy can be mates without worrying about romance . . .*

# TEST YOURSELF QUIZ

*Do you follow your school rules and regulations to the letter, or are you prepared to bend them a little? In other words, would you be the perfect prefect? Imagine yourself as one and find your true score. Maybe the job wouldn't suit you at all. Or you could be brilliant!*

# DO YOU DESERVE TO BE A PREFECT?

**1. On prefect duty at break, you find two classmates smoking a forbidden cigarette in the downstairs cloakroom. Would you . . .**
a) March them straight off to the Head to be punished?
b) Give the pair a strict warning that smoking is against school rules, and say if you catch them again you'll report it?
c) Ignore them—you don't want to cause a scene?

**2. You're supposed to supervise the canteen queue at lunchtime, but it's a sunny day and you'd rather be outside. Do you . . .**
a) Sneak off outside and leave the queue to itself?
b) Stay on duty grumpily and take it out on the hungry horde by bossing them around?
c) Stay on duty for as long as you're supposed to?

**3. It's the first day back at school after the summer hols, and you're hurrying along the corridor to get to a lesson. Then you see one of the new girls looking a bit lost and tearful. Do you . . .**
a) Sympathise and tell her she'll soon get used to it, then collar someone else to show her to her classroom?
b) Tell her to stop acting like a baby and find her class before she gets a detention for being late?
c) Ask her where she's supposed to be and take her there immediately, making yourself late?

**4. When you were a mere ordinary pupil, what did you think of the prefects?**
a) That they were just using their position to boss everyone else around?
b) That they were necessary to help both teachers and pupils to keep things running smoothly?
c) That it was their duty to maintain school discipline and order?

**5. In the playground you notice one of your fellow prefects bullying a much younger kid. What do you do?**
a) Report the incident to a teacher and insist something is done? You're very worried about it . . .
b) Think it's none of your business and walk past?
c) Go over and try to sort out the trouble between them?

**6. It's a school rule that everyone has to be outside during break. But it's a cold day, and on prefect duty you find a boy in a classroom who says he's doing extra work. Do you . .**
a) March him straight outside with everyone else? Rules are rules and mustn't be broken!
b) Turn a blind eye and hope no teacher finds him there?
c) Stay with him in the room while he finishes his work, and then make sure he goes outside?

## SCORE

| | | |
|---|---|---|
| 1 a) 5 | b) 10 | c) 0 |
| 2 a) 0 | b) 5 | c) 10 |
| 3 a) 10 | b) 5 | c) 0 |
| 4 a) 0 | b) 10 | c) 5 |
| 5 a) 10 | b) 0 | c) 5 |
| 6 a) 5 | b) 0 | c) 10 |

**WOULD YOU BE GOOD?**
50-60: Forget about being a prefect, you should be the Head!

35-45: If you're not already a prefect, you can expect to be made one very soon. And you'll be a very good prefect, too—you're prepared to be helpful and kind but at the same time you won't shirk your duties, so you'll be popular with both teachers and pupils. It's hardly all fun being a prefect, but then you wouldn't be made one unless you were trusted and thought to be responsible.

20-30: You'd make quite a good prefect, because you'd take the job very seriously. You'd see yourself as a kind of school policeman or policewoman, keeping law and order. But perhaps you'd take it a bit *too* seriously; you'd enjoy the power you had and maybe it would make you forget what it was like to be bossed about by other people. Being a prefect isn't all strictness and discipline. If you're too stern you won't win the respect of the people you're supposed to be looking after.

0-15: A very poor prefect you'd be—you wouldn't be prepared to accept the responsibility and the need to make decisions. It's a lucky prefect who isn't occasionally unpopular by making sure others keep school rules, but you'd be too timid or couldn't be bothered to do your job properly. Your classmates would know they could get away with anything when you were around. And that might land you in trouble!

## FAY LUCAS
### (Alison Bettles)

BIRTHDAY: 22nd April, 1969 STAR SIGN: Taurus
FAVOURITE FOOD: Roast beef HOBBIES: All kinds of dancing—especially modern dance, gymnastics, singing, crochet and disco roller skating
PETS: A dog called Winston BROTHERS: 2 older, Mark and Dean SISTERS: None
OTHER APPEARANCES: Lots of charity shows with Roy Hudd and other stars, a series of TV commercials for toys and record recording work

# The WOKING WONDERS!

**Paul Weller—singer, songwriter and driving force behind The Jam—hated his schooldays.**

"But the school itself," he says, "now that's a different matter. If I'd never gone to Sheerwater Comprehensive in my home town of Woking in Surrey, I might not be where I am today!"

And why is that? "Because, it was while at Sheerwater that Paul met two lads by the names of Bruce Foxton and Rick Buckler.

Who are now, of course, bass-player and drummer with The Jam.

So how exactly did they all meet up?

**BIT OF LUCK**

"Well," Paul recalls, "it was a bit of luck really. I was in a different year to Bruce and Rick, they're both a bit older than me, so in the normal run of things we might never have got together. But they were both interested in making music, and when they heard that I played guitar and had a sort of group on the go with my old mate Dave Waller, they sought me out."

Many bands form when the members meet up at school . . . and nearly as many break up when they leave to go their different ways. Not so The Jam, however—they've been a trio for some time and have stuck together!

And very soon after their first classroom meeting, the three Woking wonders got together for their first jam session.

"When we first started," says Paul, "we never seemed to play any proper songs or even to rehearse seriously. All we ever seemed to do *was* to jam. Which is how the name came about."

But although those early efforts were clumsy, and success still a long way off, Paul soon realised that making music was the one thing he really wanted to do with his life.

"It was all I ever thought about," he says. "I wasn't in the least bit interested in all the other stuff the teachers were trying to get me to learn. Looking back on it, I have to admit that I was something of a terror at school. I was always trying to get off lessons—unlike the other two, the swots!"

And, in fact, those two swots—Bruce and Rick—were doing quite well. Rick even had ambitions to be an architect, and his exam reports showed that he had the talent and the skill—but both he and Bruce became infected by "Weller's disease" and their classwork suffered.

Like Paul, music took over their lives.

"It makes me mad to think about it even now," says Paul, speaking of the fact that The Jam never received any real encouragement or help from their teachers at Sheerwater.

**EARLY GIGS**

"They didn't know how to react to people who wanted to do something other than the stuff on the syllabus,and even though we were getting better, and I could talk about music as something that I was actually good at, the teachers just didn't want to know."

They didn't want to know, either, when it was suggested that The Jam play a gig at the school.

"No-one would consider the idea," says Paul, "so we had to do all our early gigs at youth clubs and working-men's clubs."

### SAYING GOODBYE

As their talents grew, it became even more obvious that all three members of The Jam would end up in the music business in one way or another.

For Paul, being at school became a matter of waiting out his time until his sixteenth birthday—when he could say goodbye to Sheerwater for ever and finally got stuck into doing something serious that really interested him.

"I tried to keep my interest up," he says, "like in English, for instance. I didn't mind that subject at all. I love to read—and, of course, I write. But the stuff I was into was all modern by up-to-date writers.

"All my teachers kept going on about in English were people like Dickens. I suppose he's all right really—but I couldn't see what the stuff he wrote had to do with modern youth!"

And that was the attitude which inspired Paul to write material which he felt was in touch with the modern world like the song *Modern World* itself.

Another of the The Jam's big hits was *David Watts*—their version of a number originally recorded back in the 1960s by The Kinks.

"And the reason we decided to do it," Paul explains, "was just so I could get back at a boy at Sheerwater, who was just the kind of goody-goody, superior person that David Watts is in the song!".

Paul grins. "No," he says, "I won't tell you the boy's name—but he knows who I mean, all right."

And if it helps that hapless person any further to recognise himself, Paul adds that: "The last time I heard anything about him, he'd become a policeman! I'm sure he's very happy."

### WORK MEANT MONEY

Being a policeman is one of the few jobs Paul didn't do when he finally left Sheerwater at 16, with one C.S.E. to his credit. The hours wouldn't have suited!

"I was a window cleaner for a while," he recalls, "a builder . . . you name it, I did it. The main thing was that I was bringing in a bit of money and that meant that I could afford to keep the band going. Guitars and sound equipment don't just grow on trees, you know! They really eat up cash very quickly".

### BIG FOLLOWING

Bruce and Rick were only too aware of this fact as well, and that prompted them to leave school before taking their A-levels at the end of the sixth form.

Rick worked for a time as an electrical inspector, while Bruce did more or less anything that came along. Just as Paul had been doing on his own for some time.

And through all this, The Jam continued to do the rounds of the clubs and pubs in the Woking area, building up a sizeable following. Their style of music was catching on.

When they played an open-air gig on a Saturday morning in 1976, at London's Soho market, they really took off—and haven't looked back since.

Except, occasionally, to think the odd fond thought about good old Sheerwater Comprehensive!

**THE GRANGE HILL INTERVIEW**

# POGO BOUNCES ON!

**What's small, round and has a ginger topping? Pogo Patterson, of course! And Peter Moran fits exactly the same description. As for personality however, there's no similarity at all. For one thing, Peter's too busy to be thinking of sharp deals!**

**All the fictional characters in *Grange Hill* would probably agree that Pogo Patterson is a real budding con man! He never misses a chance to make a quick and easy profit—usually at someone else's expense . . .**

"I'm not a bit like that though," Peter Moran explains. And playing Pogo so well hasn't even rubbed off a bit on this freckle-faced actor. "I don't go around looking for ways of wheedling my mates' money out of them. Perhaps I could start trying, though . . ." he jokes.

Actually, it might do his friends a lot of good if Peter *did* get his hands on their money for some financial enterprise—he's a whizz kid at maths!

"Well, I'm quite good," he says modestly, "but I wouldn't go so far as to say I'm brilliant!"

Peter makes it quite clear that he's got absolutely no intention of using his mates to get into the wheeling-dealing habits that are so much a part of Pogo's personality. Quite the reverse, in fact. When recording each series is over, Peter's more than happy to leave Pogo behind on the empty set.

But it seems not everyone wants to let him put away his "screen face".

"It drives me mad," he complains. "Lots of kids are really friendly until

they discover that *I'm* not *Pogo*. Once they find out I'm normal and ordinary, they don't really want to know me any more.

### "If I met Pogo, I'd run the other way"

"The strangest thing is that I can't work out why they're so keen to get to know *him* at all. Personally, if I met Pogo, I'd check my money was still in my pocket and run the other way!"

So if financial wizardry wouldn't be Peter's scene, what would?

"Computers!" he surprises everyone by saying.

It sounds like an unusual choice for an acting type, but Peter disagrees.

"Basically, I like learning and finding out how things work. I do a lot of that in *Grange Hill*. I enjoy seeing how all the bits that we do come together to shape up into a complete programme and series. Computers are a bit like that."

Nobody's arguing with him, but then that's not a good idea anyway. As well as working out mathematical shapes, Peter spends time working out his own special shape at a local judo club!

"My instructor's terrific. He's more like a friend really, and he really inspires me to try my best. At the moment I'm a green belt and I'm hoping to go for my blue soon. Plus, of course, it's a good way to watch my weight. In case you haven't noticed, I'm what you might call on the portly side. Judo keeps me fit!"

Ski-ing also helps Pogo keep in good shape, even though some people might think it a dangerous sport for an actor to pursue. Isn't he afraid of falling and ending up with two broken legs?

"You must be joking! With the *Grange Hill* jinx on me, I'm much safer away from the studio!"

You'll probably remember that the programme's mysterious curse has already been responsible for one broken arm for Peter—and a nasty bout of chicken pox as well! Funny that he's the only one it affects!

"I tell you, I feel quite okay on skis. That is, unless my mum is near me—she's useless and likely to kill anything in her path!"

So is it Peter's dad who's the expert?

"That's right. Dad was in the army, in Germany, and that's where he picked it up. We usually go ski-ing once a year, usually Scotland or Italy—but I think Mum's decided

she's staying at home from now on—she can't stand it!"

Home for Peter is a pub in Chelsea which his parents manage.

"It's a good life running your own pub, you meet lots of different people—but I wouldn't fancy the idea myself. Mum and Dad get hardly any free time. They're working from nine in the morning till long after the place has shut. They like it—but I think it's too much like hard work."

Then does the hard work get passed on to him?

### "I'd help out at home if they gave me a couple of quid"

"No fear!" Peter protested. "I mean, I do things around the house, but I reckon that Mum and Dad pay other people to do certain chores, so I can't see why I should be free! Now, if we came to an arrangement, that would be different . . . I'd help out if they gave me a couple of quid!

"Besides, Mum and Dad understand that I've got a lot on my plate with school work and *Grange Hill*. Mum was an actress for a short time—she knows what it's like."

Peter realises his Mum's acting career didn't last long, so does he worry about the uncertainty of his own life under the spotlights?

"Well, I know it's a very risky business. I've had that luck so far, but who knows? I'd say I've got a medium chance of staying on top."

We reckon Peter's underrating himself, and we're sure if Pogo was working out the odds of him continuing in showbiz, he'd say it was a pretty safe bet!

## ROLAND BROWNING
### (Erkan Mustafa)

BIRTHDAY: 14th May, 1970 STAR SIGN: Taurus FAVOURITE FOOD: Pizzas HOBBIES: Judo, fishing and roller skating
PETS: A tortoise called Joey BROTHERS: 1 older, Martin SISTERS: 1 older, Susan
OTHER APPEARANCES: None! Erkan took his role in *Grange Hill* after being found during a nationwide search. His teacher at school suggested he auditioned for the series

# GRAFFITI!

Can't resist writing on school walls? You shouldn't, but it seems some of your teachers have exactly the same problem! We found all of these little jottings in staff rooms all around the country...

## STAFF ROOM SCRIBBLES!

I HATE KIDS

4 + 3 = 8

MY CLASS ALWAYS HAVE THEIR NOSES IN BOOKS – THEY'RE MUCH CHEAPER THAN TISSUES!

These damn kids think Richard the Lion Heart was the first organ transplant...

CAN A POLYGON REALLY BE A DISAPPEARING PARROT?

2B think a contour line is a dishonest firm of travel agents, and an isobar is something you buy from an usherette in the cinema!

THE HED CAN'T SPEL!

Sez you! You stinck

My kids are a squalid bunch of spotty juvenile delinquents with the brains of a retarded orang-utan, the alertness of a stuffed sloth, and the personal freshness and charm of a rabid skunk!

Oh, stop boasting about your luck! We all know you take the top stream!

The new biology teacher has B.O.!

## WORDS ON WALLS!

Each room in a school ends up with its own particular type of graffiti. For instance...

**THE HALL NOTICE BOARD**

DO NOT LEAVE DISCARDED CHEWING GUM BEHIND THE RADIATOR!

It makes it hard to get at, and spoils the flavour!

KEEP YOUR SCHOOL TIDY stay at home!

**MUSIC ROOM**

Why's Miss Jones so quavery? SHE'S ONLY A SEMI-BREVE

**MATHS ROOM**

BoreDom² Me + U) MaTHS

**HISTORY ROOM**

GREAT CONTEST! 1st prize – a week's history course at the museum! 2nd prize – two weeks at the museum!

**BIOLOGY ROOM**

Don't listen to 'em – it was the stork!

**GEOGRAPHY ROOM**

The earth is flat

THINK OR THWIM!

**FRENCH ROOM**

FRENCH RULES – au fait?

Knock, knock! Who's there? Mr. Mr. Who? Mr. Ball-By-A-Mile!

**GYM**

Meet me under the horse if you're interested in tunnelling out!

I DIED HERE WAITING FOR THE BELL!

## MORE SCHOOL DINNER SPECIALS

**Black treacle pudding**—oil slick on the rocks
**Minestrone**—blocked sink
**Peach crumble**—goldfish funeral
**Tinned tomatoes**—heart transplants
**Prunes**—shrunken heads
**Sausages and spinach**—hand from the swamp
**Syrup tart**—dead leaves under glue
**Boiled rice**—fisherman's bait-box
**Rhubarb and fake cream**—pond weed in winter
**Ham salad**—dog tongue in special compost
**Sharp apples**—Granny Smith's bombs
**Mushroom quiche**—open toadstool pie
**Chilli con carne**—hot mince with beetles
**Plain omlette**—fried chamois leather
**Macaroni cheese**—chopped brain surprise
**Raspberry yoghurt**—pip dip
**Egg sandwich**—yellow peril
**Corned beef**—squashed rat

## THE CANTEEN MENU BOARD

LIVER longline – don't touch it!

IRISH STEW in the name of the law!

MINCE PIE

PLUM PIE AND CUSTARD

NEVER MIND THIS LOT! FETCH ME A CROCODILE SANDWICH – and make it snappy!

# Putting you in the

## *We asked Grange Hill's John Godfrey to give us his view of life as a cameraman!*

**The fifth series of *Grange Hill* was John's first stint of working on the series, but he quickly caught the infectious enthusiasm that affects everyone who's connected with it!**

"I've never worked alongside so many kids since I was one myself," John joked. "And although that was a few years ago, the memories come flooding back!

"Work time on *Grange Hill* is like those great last weeks of term at school, where everyone's still doing their bit—but there's a holiday atmosphere.

"And I've never worked such regular hours since I was at school either," John added. "Nine to five is absolute luxury for me!"

As a full-time BBC cameraman, John travels the country working on an amazing range of programmes—dramas, documentaries—the lot!

"And the day can often start at dawn and go on until the early hours!" he told us.

"That's why it's a definite advantage working with a very young cast, the majority of whom are under sixteen. By law we can't over-run and exceed the hours they are allowed to work. We have to stop when the allotted time is up and go home!"

Before John actually started work on *Grange Hill,* he admitted that he was afraid reasonable hours would be the *only* advantage!

"I have great admiration for the theatrical profession," John sighed, "but I'm not actually very keen on actors!"

John went on to explain that he wasn't writing off all actors—just the self-centred kind!

So he was probably even more worried by the thought of child actors, we suggested. Traditionally, they're the most spoilt of their kind!

★★★★★★★★★★★★★★

***"I'm not actually very keen on actors! A lot are self centred."***

★★★★★★★★★★★★★★

"You're right. But I was wrong! I admit it. The *Grange Hill* kids aren't at all like that.

"They're very professional and sometimes it's hard to remember that they are *only* kids . . . When I get annoyed, for example!

"It's difficult. When I find that they aren't concentrating as much as I'd wish, I have to remind myself that there are so many distractions around their attention is bound to wander.

"At the end of the day though," John confessed with a smile, "I sometimes feel more like a teacher than a cameraman!"

So, as we knew how John's days end, we wanted to know how they started, too.

"Work-wise it starts the night before, actually," John laughed. "I go through the script that's to be shot the next day. I talk to the Director about the sort of effects he wants to create, where he wants the camera to be looking, etc. Then I work out the best sort of lighting.

★★★★★★★★★★★★★★

***"I sometimes feel more like a teacher than a cameraman! It's difficult . . ."***

★★★★★★★★★★★★★★

"Then if that's all done, the only thing I have to do before we start at nine is to charge my batteries with bubble and squeak in the studio canteen!"

Once everyone is in position for the day's filming, John and his close assistant, Andrew, set to it—only pausing to check that they don't run into the tea break.

# picture!

Andrew doesn't like to miss his favourite bacon roll!

John and Andrew seemed so much of a team, we wondered whether a cameraman always has the same assistant.

"We've worked together for several months," John explained. "A cameraman usually has the

★★★★★★★★★★★★★★★

***"I saved my pocket money for ages to buy my first camera—at five and sixpence."***

★★★★★★★★★★★★★★★

same crew for a short period at a time! That's the assistant cameraman and the Grips."

Just in case you're thinking the 'Grips' is some sort of wrestler-type heavy, John explained that he's the one who's responsible for looking after all the camera equipment and carting it around from place to place.

"He also brings the dolly and the rostrum and . . ."—there seemed to be no end to the list of oddly named equipment.

But, presumably, it took more than knowledge of the jargon to become a cameraman . . .

"A passion for photography *has* to be there," John explained. "All right, you need physics and

chemistry to get you through a film school course—but without the love of photography it's a complete waste of time.

"I was ten when I discovered it," John remembered. "I saved all my pocket money for ages to buy my first camera. It was called Snappie and cost five and sixpence."

"I never regretted it," he insisted. "But I do want to warn any *Grange Hill* fans who think they'd like to follow the career. It's a risky business. There isn't much work around and it can take you years to get on—even if you have been lucky enough to get a job.

"But if you can face all that," John concluded, breaking into a smile, "working in TV is a great life—and the best way of getting bubble and squeak for breakfast that I know!"

# Bluffing for Beginners!

**All right, admit it. There are some school subjects that you just can't get to grips with. You've set your heart on being a famous racing driver/master chef/property developer—and you don't see the point of studying half of the stuff you do. Well, if you've got to get through the lessons somehow, here's how to bluff the day through . . .**

## English

**Useful words to use: Shakespeare, Shelley, blank verse, Charles Dickens, onomatopoeia, adverb.**

The trouble with English teachers is that they seem to think everyone should enjoy their subject as much as they do! But if your idea of great literature is the label on the back of a sauce bottle, you're going to need a bit of help!

Sooner or later your teacher's going to ask you to prove your genius by writing something. If you're lucky, it'll be an essay, but if not, it'll be the dreaded poem!

But don't lie awake worrying about which words rhyme with what. Ten minutes before the lesson, just jot down as many nouns and verbs as you can think of—about two words to a line. It doesn't matter if they don't rhyme—or even make sense! Then, when the lesson comes, present your work to the teacher, saying, "I hope you like this. I based it on the work of Hans Grotzel. I'm very much influenced by the modern poets, you know."

After that little introduction, Teach will probably be too embarrassed to admit she doesn't understand a word of it—or know who Hans is. Who's to split that he's your pet mouse?

## Maths

**Useful words to use: algebraic equations, graphic equivalents, square roots, logarithmic.**

It's quite hard to bluff your way through a tricky subject like maths. But with a bit of practice, you can confuse your teacher into thinking he's got another Einstein in his class! Lucky thing!

Teachers like to set little problems based on everyday life. You know the kind of thing... 'If five men wanted to build a house fifty feet long by thirty five high, and it took twelve men two days to build it...' by which time you've probably fallen asleep or become very, very worried.

Well, if your teacher picks on you to answer the question, don't panic. Just keep calm, and ask, "I'm sorry, but could you tell me how tall these men are? Only it makes a lot of difference to my calculations. What with individual capacity and all that—I have to take it into account."

If you actually get a sensible answer to that one, spend the next ten minutes scribbling frantically on a scrap of paper—it doesn't matter what you put, as long as you look serious! Then you look up again and say, "How many decimal places would you like the answer to reach?" Whatever number Teach answers, sigh heavily and make it look as if you're scrubbing something out. Then start scribbling again. Keep your forehead knotted in a deep frown.

After twenty minutes, he will have given up—or dozed off! Either way, you'll be out of trouble!

## History

**Useful words to use: Napoleon, Lenin, Reformation, Renaissance, Oliver Cromwell.**

History teachers really love detail, and it's hard to bluff your way through a lesson without doing a bit of work first!

But that doesn't mean you have to learn your history book from cover to cover. Just learn as much as you can about one period in history—the less well-known the better!

Then, when your teacher picks on you and asks, "What was the name of Henry VIII's first wife?" and you give the wrong answer, you can then add, "Oh, sorry, did you say Henry VIII? I thought you meant Harold, who was killed in 1066 at Hastings by William I, King of Normandy and future King of England..." or whatever topic it is you've swotted up on! That way your teacher will either realise you're side-tracking or be very impressed! It's worth a try!

## Science

**Useful words to use: bunsen-burner, Faraday's Law, Van de Graaf generator, sulphuric acid.**

Science teachers are usually a pretty eccentric lot—but the trouble is, they do know their stuff! Well, they wouldn't be teachers otherwise, would they? So if you really don't know anything about science, keep out of your teacher's way!

Gaze seriously into your text book whenever you think you're being watched, and be seen to make frantic notes in your note-book whenever your teacher's talking. That way you'll get the reputation as being the most studious pupil in the class!

But if the worst happens and he does happen to catch you sticking a test tube up your mate's left nostril, don't panic. Just smile and explain, "You see, Sir, I was just testing out Finkelgruber's Theory of Relative Combustion—it's really quite fascinating!"

## Art

**Useful words to use: Picasso, abstract, cubist, Monet, perspective.**

Chances are the first thing your art teacher will do is ask you to draw something—usually the view out of the window. If this happens, make sure you pick yourself a good window—preferably the one where you can't see anything except a bit of sky!

If your teacher makes you draw something a bit more complicated—like a picture of your mate—and you make a mess of it, don't worry. Say it's in the style of Dali!

IT'S MY PARTY
On Friday afternoon, Sooty Sutcliffe had a job on his hands . . .
A Grange Hill Story
AH, GIRLS! GOOD JOB I CAUGHT YOU! HOW ABOUT BUYING THE LAST COUPLE OF TICKETS FOR TONIGHT'S SCHOOL DANCE?
LAST COUPLE OF DOZEN, YOU MEAN!
SORRY, SIR, WE CAN'T MAKE IT. WE'VE GOT SOMETHING ELSE ON!
A PARTY AT MY PLACE!
YOU CAN COME ALONG IF YOU LIKE!
HMPH! I MIGHT TAKE YOU UP ON THAT, THE WAY THINGS ARE GOING!
I DON'T KNOW WHAT YOUR BROTHER WOULD SAY IF SOOTY DID TURN UP! HE PROBABLY DOESN'T EVEN WANT US THERE . . .
HE DOESN'T! SAID I OUGHT TO SPEND THE NIGHT AT YOUR PLACE.

BUT I THREATENED TO TELL DAD ABOUT THE PARTY IF HE DIDN'T LET US COME!
ANYWAY, YOU'VE OKAYED IT WITH YOUR MUM?
YES! OF COURSE, SHE DOESN'T KNOW YOUR MUM AND DAD WON'T BE THERE!
HOW LONG WILL THEY BE AWAY?
JUST OVERNIGHT, THEY'RE VISITING MY AUNTIE. LONG ENOUGH FOR US TO HAVE A GOOD TIME, THOUGH!
Several stops later . . .
SEE YOU ABOUT EIGHT! DON'T FORGET TO BRING THOSE RECORDS!
IT'LL BE GREAT, BEING ABLE TO DO WHAT WE LIKE . . . WITH NO PARENTS TO BOSS US AROUND!
Back home . . .
WHERE HAVE YOU BEEN?
I GOT HOME AS FAST AS I COULD! MUM AND DAD GONE?

THINK I'D BRING THIS LOT IN IF THEY HADN'T?
BLIMEY, WHAT'RE YOU TRYING TO FEED . . . A WHOLE ARMY?
SLICED PAN
RITZ
OKAY, PANIC'S OVER! CAPTAIN MARVEL'S HERE!
CAW! BROOKE ROAD'S ANSWER TO SIMON BATES!
SEE YOU'VE GOT THE TALENT LINED UP ALREADY!
HI, GARY!
HEY, HANDS OFF THE LITTLE 'UN!
LESS OF THE "LITTLE 'UN", IF YOU DON'T MIND!
WAHAY! HE THINKS YOU'RE STILL IN NAPPIES!
EIGHT ON THE DOT! NOT BAD TIMING, EH!
YOU NEEDN'T HAVE RUSHED! NO-ONE'S HERE YET!
I LIKE YOUR OUTFIT! BUT IT MAKES YOU LOOK OLDER . . .
I *WANT* TO LOOK OLDER, IDIOT. THAT'S THE WHOLE POINT!

ANYWAY, WHY'S NO-ONE TURNED UP?
THEY NEVER DO 'TIL AROUND TEN! DOESN'T STOP *US* FROM DANCING, THOUGH!
"... HANDS UP, BABY, HANDS UP ..."
"... GIMME YOUR HEART, GIMME GIMME ..."
BLIMEY, HAVEN'T YOU GOT ANYTHING NEWER THAN THAT?
STOP MOANING, YOU TWO!
Two hours later ...
IF I'D KNOWN IT'D BE THIS LATE STARTING, I'D HAVE GONE TO THE SCHOOL DANCE FIRST!
YOU CAN ALWAYS GO TO BED IF IT'S PAST YOUR BEDTIME!
DING DONG!!
AHA! HERE THEY COME! WE HAVE LIFT-OFF!
WOTCHER, DAN! TOLD YA WE'D FIND IT SOONER OR LATER!
AMAZING! PEOPLE ARE ACTUALLY STARTING TO ARRIVE!
Soon ...
BLIMEY, WHERE'D THEY ALL COME FROM?
EH? WHAT?
"... I WAS WORKING AS A WAITRESS IN A COCKTAIL BAR ..."

HEY, WATCH OUT!. . . GAAH!
'SCUSE ME!
SPLOSH!
STUPID GREAT CLOWN! I'M SOAKED!
THERE'S A CLOTH IN THE KITCHEN!
COME LOOKING FOR US, HAVE YA?
ONLY IF YOU HAPPEN TO BE A DISH-CLOTH!
LIKE US TO GET YOU A DRINK?
NO THANKS!
HELLO . . . WHAT'S THIS YOU TWO ARE DRINKING?
COKE! IF YOU MUST KNOW!
THAT'S ALL IT'D BETTER BE!
A BIT YOUNG TO BE YOUR DAD, ISN'T HE?
SATISFIED?
YEAH . . . BUT I'M KEEPING AN EYE ON YOU!
WANNA DANCE?

I WISH HE'D SHOVE OFF. HE'S AS BAD AS MUM AND DAD.
WHO'D YOU THINK YOU ARE?
COME ON! YOU CAN LEAVE THAT OUT!
I'M HER BROTHER! AND I DON'T REMEMBER INVITING YOU TWO!
BLIMEY, HE'S WORSE THAN OLD CLARKEY AT SCHOOL!
STOP TREATING US LIKE KIDS!
LOOK, I'M NOT GETTING THE BLAME IF ANYTHING HAPPENS TO YOU!
So . . .
HMPH! FAT CHANCE THERE IS OF ANYTHING EXCITING HAPPENING AFTER HE'S STUCK HIS FACE IN!
NO-ONE'S EVEN ASKING US TO DANCE!
HEY, YOU'D BETTER GO AND SEE TO YOUR BROTHER!
WHAT? WHAT'S WRONG WITH HIM?
HE'S NOT FEELING TOO WELL!
I THINK SOMEONE'S MIXED HIS DRINKS!

NOW, I WONDER HOW THAT COULD HAVE HAPPENED . . .
THOSE TWO! IT'D BE JUST LIKE THEM . . .
DANNY! WAKE UP!
IT'S NO USE! HE'LL BE OUT FOR HOURS!
BLIMEY, THAT LEAVES ME IN CHARGE OF THE PARTY!
WELL . . . WE WERE GETTING A BIT CHEESED OFF WITH HIS NOSING!
YEAH, BUT WHAT IF SOMETHING HAPPENS . . . SOMETHING GETS DAMAGED . . . OR THERE'S A FIGHT?
I THOUGHT WE WERE HERE TO ENJOY OURSELVES!
HOW ABOUT THAT DANCE THEN, GIRLS . . . NOW THAT BIG BROTHER'S OUT OF THE WAY!
WELL, IF YOU . . .
ER, NO THANKS! NOT JUST NOW!
HE'S PLAYING ONE OF MY RECORDS — LET'S DANCE!
But, suddenly . . .
LOOK OUT!
ZZZZZ
OH, NO! . . . THOSE CLOWNS HAVE SCRATCHED IT!

LOOK AT THAT . . . RIGHT ACROSS!
SORRY, I TOLD THEM BEFORE NOT TO DANCE SO CLOSE!
DING DONG
DOORBELL!
GAAH! WHO SPILT THAT? MY MUM'LL KILL US!
DING DONG!!
DING DONG!!
I'M COMING, I'M COMING!
SURELY, PEOPLE CAN'T BE TURNING UP THIS LATE!
DON'T YOU LOT REALISE WHAT TIME IT IS? PEOPLE ARE TRYING TO SLEEP!
CUT OUT THE RACKET, OR WE'LL CALL THE POLICE!
HEY, GARY! . . . BETTER TURN THAT THING DOWN! THE NEIGHBOURS ARE COMPLAINING!
IGNORE THEM!
SIGH! FIRST WE'D TROUBLE GETTING THEM TO COME . . . NOW WE CAN'T GET RID OF THEM!
I'M GOING TO DROP OFF TO SLEEP ANY MINUTE!
CAN'T SLEEP IN MY ROOM! THERE'S PEOPLE KIPPING ALL OVER THE PLACE! GRAB THESE!
YAWN! DON'T WORRY, I COULD SLEEP STANDING UP!

'NIGHT!
MMFF!
Then suddenly . . .
WAKEY, WAKEY!
UH? . . . OHHH, IT'S NOT MORNING ALREADY, IS IT?
HECK! IT'S ELEVEN O'CLOCK!
WHAT!! MUM AND DAD'LL BE BACK SOON!
LOOK AT THE STATE OF THIS PLACE!
HEY, AREN'T YOU GOING TO HELP US TO CLEAR UP?
SORRY, GOTTA GO!
So, guess who got lumbered . . .
PAH! IT'S ALL RIGHT FOR DANNY! HE'S STILL OUT FOR THE COUNT!
KEEP UP THE GOOD WORK, GIRLS! SEE YA!
PHEW! FINISHED! YOUR PARENTS CAN COME HOME ANY TIME THEY LIKE NOW!
JUST AS LONG AS THEY DON'T SPEAK TO ANY NEIGHBOURS!

OH! TIDIED 'UP, HAVE YOU? I WAS GONNA GIVE YOU A HAND!
OH YEAH?!
THAT'S TYPICAL OF HIM! LAZY SLOB!
LET'S TAKE A WALK AND TRY TO FORGET ALL ABOUT IT!
HEY, SUZANNE! HOW'D IT GO LAST NIGHT?
GROAN! PRECIOUS MATTHEWS! TRUST US TO BUMP INTO HER!
I GOT LUMBERED INTO GOING TO THE DANCE!
THE PARTY WAS GREAT! WASN'T IT, CLAIRE?
ER . . . OH, YEAH . . . FANTASTIC! WHAT DID WE MISS?
OH NOTHING. THE USUAL – SOOTY FELL OVER MOONEY, BAXTER DROOLED OVER LEXY AND GRIPPER STEBSON GOT CHUCKED OUT! APART FROM THAT, NOTHING MUCH HAPPENED!
BET YOU'RE GLAD YOU DIDN'T GO!
I DON'T KNOW ABOUT THAT!
SOUNDS LIKE PARADISE COMPARED WITH WHAT WE'VE BEEN THROUGH!
THE END